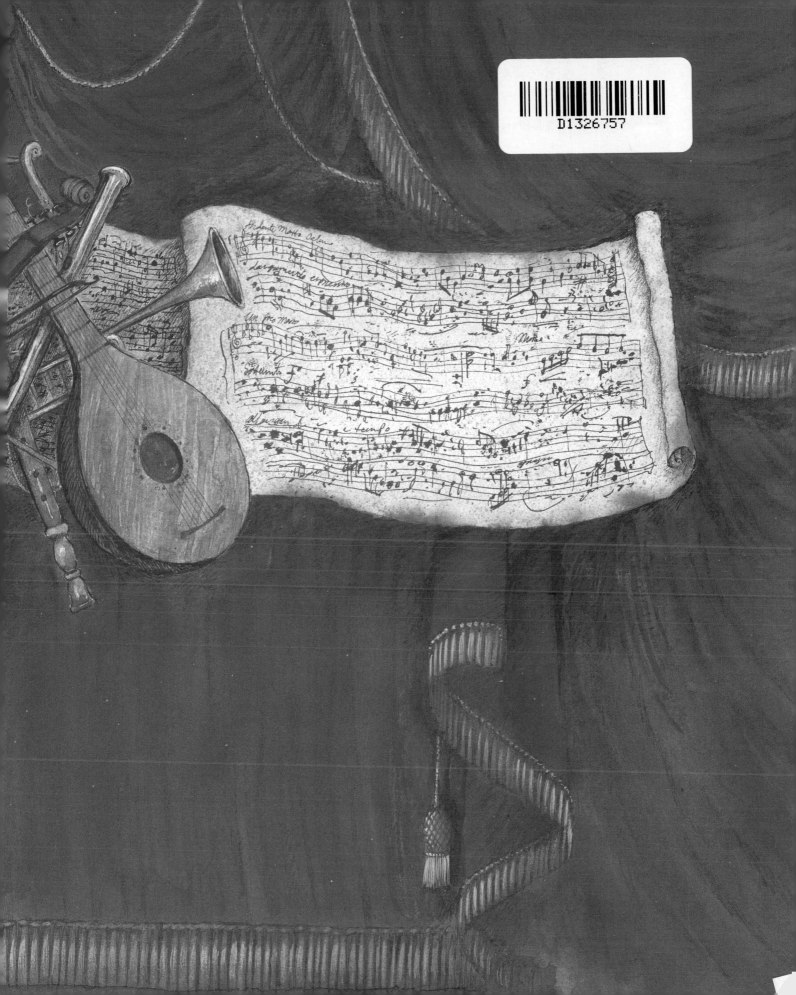

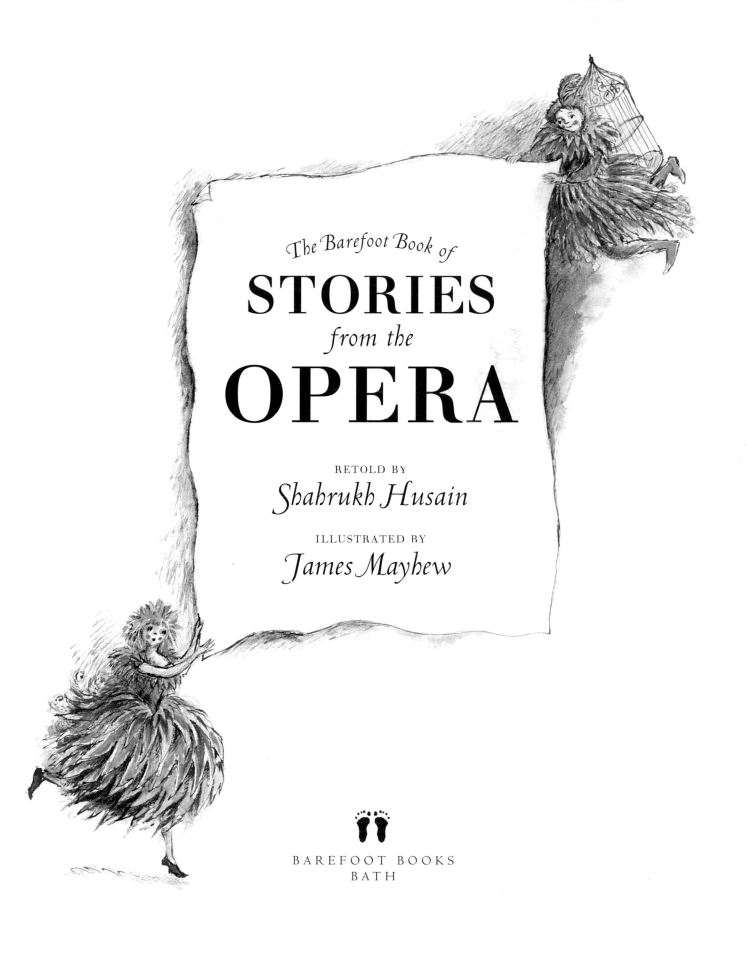

The Barefoot Book of

STORIES
from the
OPERA

RETOLD BY
Shahrukh Husain

ILLUSTRATED BY
James Mayhew

BAREFOOT BOOKS
BATH

Barefoot Collections
an imprint of
Barefoot Books
PO Box 95
Kingswood
Bristol
BS30 5BH

First published in Great Britain in 1999 by Barefoot Books Ltd

The main text has been typeset in Monotype Centaur roman, 13pt on 18pt leading
The illustrations were prepared in watercolour and pen and ink on watercolour paper

This book has been printed on 100% acid-free paper

Graphic design by Design/Section, Frome
Colour separation by Grafiscan, Verona
Printed and bound in Hong Kong by South China Printing Co. (1988) Ltd

ISBN I 901223 41 8

British Library Cataloguing-in-Publication Data:
a catalogue record for this book is available from the British Library

3 5 7 9 8 6 4 2

Contents

Introduction

Did you know that, once upon a time, myths and fairy tales were recited and written for adults rather than for children? Well, they were. That is why they were made into plays, which were watched by royalty, warriors and the general public from ancient times.

Since then, singing has been an important part of drama. But opera, as we know it today, was created in Florence in Italy, at the beginning of the seventeenth century, when certain kinds of comedy and spectacular masked performances began to make lavish use of music. In opera, this love of music went a step further – even the dialogue in the play was set to tunes. Myths, such as *Orpheus and Eurydice* in this book, were popular in opera too, as were fairy tales and folk tales.

For the first thirty or so years, opera was performed mainly in private for the wealthy. Then, in 1637, the first public theatre was built in Venice. Suddenly, opera became available to the general public and new ones were written in France, Austria, Germany and England. Since then, it has become popular all over the world. Sometimes English-speaking opera companies translate the libretto (the script) of French, German or Italian operas into English. But more often the operas are performed with the libretto in its original language.

It does not matter if you do not understand the words because music, if you listen attentively, has a language of its own. But you may find it helpful to read a summary of the story before watching. Or, if you have the time, you can read an English translation of the libretto. This is not always written by the person who composes the music, though certain composers, such as Wagner and Rimsky-Korsakov, did write the stories as well.

Whether or not the composer wrote the libretto, he was given the greater importance. After all, he wrote the music that lifted the story out of its ordinary setting and placed it in the grand world of opera. Today, the sets are more splendid than ever before, the orchestras better and the choruses are very carefully trained. Some opera singers are famous and highly paid, not surprisingly, since they study for years until their voices become like perfectly tuned instruments. The tough preparation turns them into skilful actors as well. They have to use their voices and faces to express the feelings of the characters they are playing. You can imagine how hard they work!

As you can see, the opera is a rich and exciting world and there is much to learn about it. For me, the quickest way to get involved in an opera is to read the story. Knowing the characters helps me to understand the meaning and moods of the music and to appreciate just how well it suits the words.

I hope that the stories here will make the opera as exciting for you as it always is for me.

Shahrukh Husain

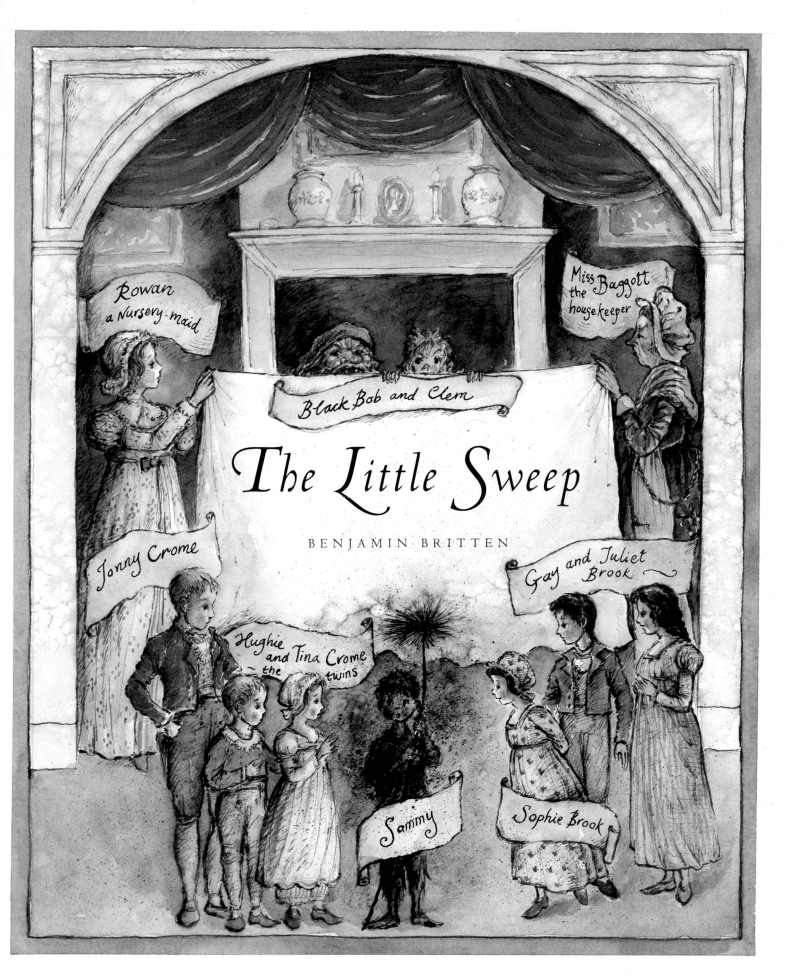

Benjamin
Britten
1913 ~ 1976

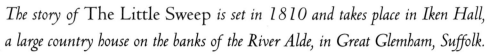

The story of The Little Sweep *is set in 1810 and takes place in Iken Hall, a large country house on the banks of the River Alde, in Great Glemham, Suffolk.*

In those days log-fires warmed the rooms and everyone had to have their chimneys regularly cleaned. If they didn't, the soot would block the chimneys and the rooms would soon fill with smoke.

Cleaning chimneys was specialised work, but very unpleasant, messy and uncomfortable. It was left to chimney sweeps who were generally blackened with soot from head to toe, clothes and all! That — and a cruel nature — earned the chief sweep in this opera the title of Black Bob. Like most sweeps, he used a small boy to scrape and scrub inside the chimney flues, which were usually far too narrow to fit a grown man. Imagine climbing inside a long, narrow chimney flue, struggling to keep a foot-hold on the rungs flattened against the inside wall, while trying to loosen the thick soot collected there. The boy would be terrified of losing his footing and falling off as the soot fell in his eyes or he breathed it up his nose and mouth. It was quite horrible.

Understandably, not many children wanted to work as a sweep's boy, but times were hard. If there was no work, the poor were in danger of being turned out of their lodgings or dying of cold or starvation. So parents sold their sons to the sweeps for a few years in return for a little money to live on. They hoped that the sweep would look after their children and teach them the job kindly and patiently. Some boys were treated well, but others, like Sammy in this story, were treated very badly and longed to escape.

Benjamin Britten was the first composer ever to be made a lord for his work. His opera, Peter Grimes, *changed completely the way English opera was written. He founded the Aldeburgh Music Festival in 1948, and* The Little Sweep *was first performed there in the same year.*

The Little Sweep

BENJAMIN BRITTEN

Black Bob, the chimney sweep, and his son Clem were on their way to Iken Hall, the home of Mr and Mrs Brook and their three children, Juliet, Sophie and their brother Gay. And what a grubby, sullen pair they were as they walked along with their ropes, brushes and sacks. They jeered at little Sammy who was trying desperately to keep up with them. The huge rope, which Bob had slung across from Sammy's shoulder to his waist, rubbed his neck painfully, and his small arms could barely hold the three baskets full of brushes and cleaning things he had to carry.

Sammy was only eight years old. His grimy little face was ashen and unhappy and tears coursed down, leaving pale channels on his cheeks. You see, Sammy had only recently come to work for Black Bob and today, for the first time ever, he would be pushed up the filthy, dark chimney-stacks. There were seven chimneys at Iken Hall – all of them tall and narrow – and Sammy was frightened. But instead of preparing Sammy kindly for the job, Bob and Clem taunted, teased and scared him even more.

When the sweeps arrived, they were sent up to the nursery where Miss Baggott, the housekeeper, was waiting.

'Hurry, Rowan!' she barked at the nursery-maid who had brought Jonny, Hughie and Tina Crome on a visit to the Brook family. 'Don't stand there staring, girl, get on with it. And you,' she said, turning to the three sweeps as they walked in, 'don't you dare spread your filth around here!'

Rowan flung the last white sheet over the furniture to protect it from the soot. She was impatient to get away from Miss Baggott and join the children who were playing downstairs. As she turned, her eyes fell on Sammy who she could see had been crying.

7

'Poor little chap,' she thought, 'skinny as a scarecrow. And those clothes! So tattered and patched.'

But what could she do? She was only here as a guest and as nursery-maid to the Crome children. Sadly, she slipped out of the door, leaving the sweeps to begin their work.

Black Bob's eyes glinted as he towered over Sammy. 'Shivering with fright, eh, little boy?' he mocked. 'You might well be – it's time for your climb.'

He reached out and grabbed Sammy by the waist. Together he and Clem shoved him up inside the chimney. Sammy's foot groped for the first rung of the ladder.

'Get up and get cleaning,' boomed Bob, menacingly, 'or I'll cook you alive!'

Sammy scrambled up the ladder in panic.

'Make sure you do a proper job – little scraper and sack boy!' yelled Clem, as Sammy's feet vanished up the flue. Then he followed Bob out of the nursery to check the next chimney on the list.

The children were playing hide-and-seek. As soon as Juliet saw the sweeps leave the nursery, she nipped in and hid herself in a chair beneath the sheets. A moment later, Hughie and Tina burst in.

'She's not here,' they said, disappearing as fast as they had appeared. Juliet poked her head out from underneath the sheet and then withdrew quickly as Jonny put his head round the door.

'Caught you,' he said, lifting the sheet.

'Quick, Jonny,' said Juliet, 'you hide too. There's loads of room here.' Jonny settled himself beside Juliet and they pulled the sheet back over again, giggling as they heard the others shouting for them.

But who was that? Someone was calling for help. And the call was coming from very near them. Juliet and Jonny threw off the sheet and looked around. The rope in the fireplace shuddered violently.

'Help me, please, I can't move!' came a faint voice.

'Who is it?' called Juliet and Jonny together.

'Please get me down,' came the voice again.

'The sweep boy!' yelled Juliet. 'He's stuck in the chimney!'

Juliet turned to Jonny. 'We're going to need help. Get the others.'

'Help me. I can't breathe,' wailed Sammy from up the chimney.

The other children exploded into the nursery with Jonny.

Juliet grasped the rope. 'We have to get him down,' she said. 'NOW!'
The children huddled in the fireplace holding the rope tight.

'Are you ready, Sammy?' Juliet asked.

'Yes,' replied Sammy.

They tugged gently on the rope but Sammy didn't budge.

'It's no good,' he sobbed.

'Pull harder,' said Juliet. 'But don't yank.'

They did as she said, but Sammy remained firmly wedged in the flue.

'Try again,' said Juliet. 'One, two, three. Pull!'

This time, the rope gave and Sammy came howling down in a black shower
of soot and stones. He lay very still on the hearth.

'He's dead!' cried the twins as the children gathered around, all speaking
at once.

'Are you hurt?'

'We're very sorry.'

'We just wanted to help.'

'Don't make me go back up,' whimpered Sammy. 'Please don't.'

'Poor thing!' said the children, all speaking together again. 'He's so little.'

'He looks so weak, and scared.'

'Please don't make me go back up,' begged Sammy again.

'Will Miss Baggott let him stay?' wondered the children. Then they decided
that she would not. Even worse, she would probably return him to Black Bob.

'Please don't make me go back up,' Sammy repeated as the others tried to
think how they could save him.

'Please don't ... '

'We won't tell anyone about you, Sammy,' they said together.

'You can hide among our toys,' said Gay.

'Yes, there's plenty of room for you,' Jonny agreed.

'Be quick!'

'Wait a moment,' said Juliet, 'we've got to make them think he's run away, or they'll find him.'

Sophie pointed to the window. If Sammy went through it and down the creeper, the grown-ups would think he had run away. Sophie led him to the window, making sure he left black foot-tracks across the white sheets. Sammy took off his shoes and socks and waited to be told what to do next.

Thump. Thump. Thump. Miss Baggott's footsteps approached the nursery.

The children pounced on Sammy and pushed him into the cupboard before dashing under the sheets. Miss Baggott walked into the room followed by Bob and Clem. What a mess!

'Why aren't the chimneys done yet, you idle good-for-nothings?' she demanded.

'She does bark on, doesn't she?' grumbled Black Bob, under his breath. 'Real old bossy-boots, I call her,' muttered Clem.

But Miss Baggott was too busy looking around to notice their scowling faces. 'The window's open,' she exclaimed suddenly, her eyes bulging.

The children's plan was working! Sooty footprints, leading to the open window, told the grown-ups that Sammy had run away.

'After him!' shouted Bob and Clem, dashing through the door, threatening to chain Sammy up with the dog or lock him in the chicken coop and whip him.

'Come back!' screeched Miss Baggott, racing after the sweeps. 'You useless scoundrels. You have six more chimneys to clean.'

When the dust had settled, kind-hearted Rowan leaned out of the window, silently urging Sammy on. As the sweeps ran across the court-yard, Miss Baggott rushed out of the front door after them, wearing her hat, coat and walking shoes. Clearly, she meant to catch them!

'Poor, unlucky little boy,' murmured Rowan. 'Run as fast as you can.'

How cold Sammy would be out by the frozen river! Would he find a place to hide? And what would Black Bob do to him if he were found?

'I so wish I could save you!' she cried, helplessly. 'I'd hide you away safe from those awful slave-drivers.'

The children heard Rowan's words and crept out from under the sheet.

'We knew you would be on our side,' whispered Jonny, leading her to the toy cupboard.

'Good heavens!' cried Rowan as Sammy's sooty head popped out. 'The little sweep!'

The children clustered around Rowan, asking her to keep their secret and to help them look after the little sweep.

'Give him a bath!' yelled Hughie and Tina.

'What about Miss Baggott?' asked Sophie anxiously. But Rowan knew Miss Baggott would be out for quite a while if she intended to catch the sweeps. Suddenly everyone began to help. Rowan filled the buckets, the twins fetched down the bath from the attic, Sophie brought some clothes out of Jonny's trunk and Jonny carried in the water. Gay lit the fire and Juliet found some soap and towels. Then the children left the room so that Sammy could have his bath.

For the next few minutes, Rowan scrubbed Sammy and washed him until all the soot was off and Sammy was squeaky clean. Then she dressed him in Jonny's clothes and flung open the door.

The children looked at Sammy in amazement. They could hardly believe that the little boy standing in front of them was the grubby, miserable, half-starved little sweep of a few moments ago.

'Where are your father and mother, Sammy?' asked Juliet, wondering if they could save Sammy by sending him back to them.

'In Little Glemham,' replied Sammy.

'Little Glemham!' exclaimed Rowan. 'That's my village.'

'My father's called Sparrow. He's a waggoner.'

'Goodness me!' said Rowan. 'I know Josiah Sparrow!' Then she stopped. 'Did he sell you to Black Bob?' Sammy hung his head.

'How can you sell a person?' demanded Gay. 'Specially your own child?'

'Well,' Sammy defended his father, 'Dad broke his hip last harvest. He couldn't work and there was nothing to eat ...'

'We'd better clear up,' Rowan reminded them. 'Miss Baggott will be back soon.'

11

Instantly, they set about clearing away the bath things, but the enthusiasm they had felt about saving Sammy was replaced with worries. What a dreadful life poor Sammy had. No wonder he had been weeping when he came. Children should be able to laugh and play, like them. But not Sammy. Not since he had left home for his rotten job with the sweeps. What would become of him?

Then Jonny had an idea: 'Rowan, leave a space in my trunk when you pack,' he exclaimed. 'We can smuggle Sammy out in it.'

'But he won't be able to breathe,' protested Rowan.

'We can stop the coach and let him out when we've left Iken Hall.'

'I don't know,' said Rowan, worried. 'What will your parents think?'

'They'll let him stay,' Jonny insisted. 'Or help him and his family.'

'But where will he sleep tonight?'

'In the toy cupboard,' replied Gay.

There was no time to argue. The crunch of footsteps on the gravel warned them Miss Baggott was back.

'The nursery's still untidy!' wailed Rowan, but it was too late. Sammy leaped swiftly into the cupboard. By the time Miss Baggott arrived, the children were settled cosily around the fireplace, reading, playing board games and helping Rowan wind balls of wool.

Miss Baggott stomped into the nursery in her outdoor clothes. 'First they run off without finishing their job,' she moaned, slumping heavily into a chair. 'Then they insult me! Do you know, they accused ME of hiding their wretched boy? If I get my hands on him I'll … !'

As soon as Miss Baggott had gone, Jonny ran to the cupboard. 'Just get through tonight, Sammy,' he whispered. 'Tomorrow you'll be free.'

The next morning, Rowan brought Juliet breakfast in bed. 'You get some breakfast inside you, too,' she said, letting Sammy out of the cupboard. 'And give your legs a good stretch. You'll be in the trunk in twenty minutes.'

Sammy gobbled down his ham and eggs as Juliet unstrapped a large trunk, singing away to herself about how the coach would carry Sammy away to safety. Then she gave him three gleaming half-crowns.

'I couldn't take those,' gasped Sammy, 'I've never seen so much money.' But Juliet insisted and there was no time left to argue because the others came in and Sammy had to get into the trunk.

Once he was inside, everyone relaxed. It would be easy from now on. Old Alf, the gardener, and Tom, the coachman, were already on their way up, mumbling about their creaking joints and their aching backs. Just a few moments from now, the trunk would be on the coach and Sammy would be free.

Alf took one side of the trunk, Tom the other and they heaved. But the trunk didn't budge. They tried again. Not an inch. 'Can't lift it,' said Tom.

'Can't lift a small case full of clothes?' jeered Miss Baggott.

'Stones and sand, more like,' grumbled Tom, 'or books.'

'I know what's in it,' snapped Miss Baggott. 'I packed it!'

'Well then, you'll just have to unpack it!' retorted Alf.

'The cheek,' began Miss Baggott.

'We'll help you carry it,' Juliet blurted out.

'And so will I,' chimed in Rowan.

'Right then,' agreed Tom. 'That makes it worth a try.'

So everyone huddled around the trunk and lifted together at the count of three while Miss Baggott watched open-mouthed. And what a relief! The trunk swung up and was carried down the stairs with Miss Baggott shouting warnings after them not to scrape the paint or damage the woodwork.

A few moments later, the trunk was safely on the coach, which the Crome children boarded, waving goodbye with smiling faces. From their bedroom window, Juliet, Gay and Sophie waved back and called their farewells. 'Goodbye, Rowan. Goodbye, Jonny and Hughie and Tina!' And softly so that no one else could hear, they whispered, 'Goodbye, Sammy, have a good life.'

Three Genies

Queen of Night

Three Ladies-in-Waiting

Papageno

Papagena

The Magic Flute

WOLFGANG AMADEUS MOZART

Sarastro
High Priest
of the Sun

Monostatos –
a Moorish Slave

Tamino –
a foreign prince

Pamina –
daughter of the
Queen of Night

Wolfgang Amadeus Mozart
1756~1791

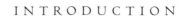

The story of The Magic Flute *unfolds long, long ago, in the secret parts of ancient Egypt. There, in a dark kingdom, surrounded by a mysterious range of mountains, the mighty Queen of Night, sometimes known as the Starry Queen, holds sway. Not far away, by the edge of the vast Egyptian desert, lives Sarastro, the powerful High Priest of a secret religion. Sarastro, much feared by his enemies, resides with his priests, surrounded by temples and gardens, in the shadow of the pyramids. As High Priest, he is in charge of the temples and the priests and rules with an iron hand.*

In Sarastro's castle is an important prisoner, guarded night and day by the horrible Captain of the Guard, Monostatos. She is Princess Pamina, the Queen of Night's daughter. Naturally, her imprisonment is the cause of a terrible feud (quarrel) between Sarastro and the queen. But there is something else that bothers the queen: Sarastro possesses the mighty Circle of the Sun, which grants all its guardian's desires. The queen wants the Circle because it belonged to her husband when he was alive but Sarastro claims it was left to him. And so the feud rages on.

Meanwhile, the queen still has a magic flute, which her husband made many years ago. The flute has amazing powers. It can soothe savage animals, calm the furious and pacify nature and the elements. When Prince Tamino agrees so readily to help her rescue Pamina from Sarastro, the queen gives him the flute to help him in his quest, for who could make a better owner than the pure-hearted prince? But Tamino has yet to learn who is fighting for Good in this feud and who is on the side of Evil.

As the opera begins, Tamino has just stumbled into the realm of the Queen of Night and meets a lot of strange and interesting people who start him on an adventure that will change his life.

Wolfgang Amadeus Mozart, who wrote the music for The Magic Flute, *started composing at the age of five and at six he was performing in front of the Empress of Austria. Although he wrote some of the world's most beautiful music, he died very poor aged only thirty-five.*

16

The Magic Flute

WOLFGANG AMADEUS MOZART

Prince Tamino found himself in a strange, bleak spot surrounded by scrub and a few odd trees. He had never before been to this part of Egypt. A giant serpent had chased him here and he looked hastily at the rocks looming up around him. Should he hide in that round temple nearby, or would a clump of trees be safer? But it was too late. Before he could decide, the serpent's poisonous tongue flicked the back of his neck and he fell down in a dead faint.

As the serpent dropped its great, drooling jaws over Tamino, three mysterious women threw open the door of the temple and approached. The serpent reared up, its body outspread, its fangs bared, guarding its prey. But the women were not afraid. They held up their silver daggers and chanted magical words until he fell down dead beside the prince, a harmless pile of coils.

Slowly, the women drew close to Tamino.

'He's handsome,' said the first.

'And he looks strong,' said the second.

'Let's tell our queen,' said the third. And they vanished through the temple doors.

Tamino opened his eyes and saw the dead serpent beside him. 'Who killed it?' he wondered. Then he heard a sound. He jumped lithely to his feet and hid behind a tree just as a feathery man pranced into the clearing, pretending to be a bird.

'Who are you?' asked Tamino, in disbelief.

'Papageno, the bird-catcher,' replied the man.

'You saved my life!' said Tamino. 'Thank you.'

'It was nothing,' muttered Papageno.

Suddenly, the temple doors flew open. 'You did not kill the serpent, you miserable specimen,' the first woman called out, 'we did.'

'It's not very nice to lie,' added the second, grabbing his cheeks.

'I'm afraid we must punish you,' said the third, pushing a gag into his mouth.

'Now,' they said, 'you can't utter a word, until you've learned what a bad thing it is to lie and to take credit for the work of others.'

With Tamino, though, the women were all smiles and charm. 'Our mistress, the Queen of Night, welcomes you to her realm,' they said showing him a portrait. 'This is Pamina, our princess.'

'I must meet her,' said Tamino, his eyes drawn like magnets to the beautiful face in the portrait.

The women grew sad. 'Pamina was kidnapped ... '

'One May night ...'

'When she was asleep under a tree.'

Tamino was horrified. 'Who took her?'

'An evil wizard called Sarastro. He has locked her up in his castle.' As they spoke, the mountains drew apart before Tamino's eyes, revealing a deep, dark chamber hung with millions of twinkling stars. In the centre, on her throne, was the Queen of Night, tall, regal and dressed all in black. 'Bring my daughter back to me,' she said, in a rich, haunting voice.

Tamino bowed low and promised to rescue Pamina. The Queen of Night thanked him and the mountains closed up again.

Poor Papageno! All he could do was squawk 'hmm-hmm' and hop around in frustration, feathers flying in all directions.

Tamino looked at him pityingly. 'I wish I could help,' he said, 'but I'm not sure how.'

'The queen has told us to do as Prince Tamino wants,' said one woman. 'But do you promise never to lie again?'

Papageno let out an ear-splitting squawk that sent Tamino's hands flying to his ears.

'Don't do that!' said one woman, hastily removing the gag. 'And go and help Tamino find the princess.'

The women gave Tamino a magic flute to help him on his journey. And to Papageno they gave a box of silver chimes, which they called a glockenspiel. Then they summoned three small genies in a flying machine to guide them to Sarastro's castle in the land of pyramids. There, guarded by Monostatos, the Captain of the Guard, and his soldiers, lived Pamina. At every chance she got, she tried to run away to get back to her mother.

That day, Pamina was tired and very fed-up because she had, once again, tried unsuccessfully to escape and was now locked up once more. Monostatos's footsteps clanged down the corridor. As usual, he would try to bully her into marrying him. He flung open the door and Pamina braced herself. But Monostatos stood frozen in the doorway, his eyes bulging. Amazed, Pamina swung round and saw he had been frightened by a large, feathery creature teetering on the window-sill. Monostatos let out a howl of fear. The feathered thing screeched back in terror. That was enough for Monostatos! He ran down the corridor as if a pack of demons was chasing him.

The feathered creature calmed down a little. 'Prince Tamino is coming to rescue you,' he stuttered. 'I'm Papageno. Your mother sent us. And here's your portrait to prove I am who I say I am and was sent by who I say sent me. Tamino loves you.'

Pamina blushed. A prince was coming to her rescue. She was so thankful, she fell in love with him immediately!

'Well,' grinned Papageno, guessing how she felt. 'What are we waiting for? Let's go and find your prince.'

Pamina's face lit up. With someone to help her, she had a better chance of escaping. Silently, she guided Papageno through tunnels and passages and soon they were on their way. But they had hardly left the castle grounds when Monostatos discovered Pamina was gone. At once, he summoned his soldiers and set out after her.

Some distance away, in the same kingdom, Tamino stood outside Sarastro's temples, confused and a little daunted. He squared his shoulders, stretched himself to his full height and tried the door to the Temple of Truth.

'Step back!' came an echoing command.

So Tamino tried the door to the Temple of Reason.

'Step back!' The voice was louder this time.

So he tried the door to the Temple of Wisdom.

This time, a priest welcomed him in. 'What are you looking for?' he asked.

'I have come to rescue Pamina,' began Tamino.

'But you've come with thoughts of anger and revenge,' the priest reproached him gently.

'Yes, but only against the evil wizard Sarastro,' argued Tamino.

The priest rubbed his chin thoughtfully. 'Hmm. I see you've been misled. The Queen of Night lied to you.'

'Then tell me the truth,' Tamino challenged.

'If you truly want to know,' replied the priest, 'you'll find out soon enough.' And with those words, he left Tamino confused, and still troubled about Pamina.

Longingly, Tamino began to play the magic flute, letting its music wash over him. As he grew peaceful, he saw the wild animals from the surrounding wilderness venture slowly out of their hiding places to sit beside him and listen. Now Tamino knew in his heart that Pamina was alive.

Not far away, Pamina and Papageno heard the plaintive call of Tamino's flute as they dodged and dived to stay safe from Monostatos and his pursuing soldiers. Papageno pulled out his chimes and answered Tamino.

'We're lost,' whispered Pamina, as Monostatos's men surrounded them. 'Now we'll both be prisoners.'

'Maybe,' replied Papageno, 'but not before we've had some fun.'

As he spoke, the soldiers closed in on them, grim and serious. Monostatos came nearer, baring his teeth and growling like a crazed animal. Gaily, Papageno struck the chimes. As the notes fell on their ears, the soldiers began to twitch and fidget. Their arms and legs jerked and their swords and daggers flew off their twirling bodies. What a sight! Papageno and Pamina laughed uncontrollably, watching the soldiers' expressions change from surprise to rage as their bodies danced on with a will of their own.

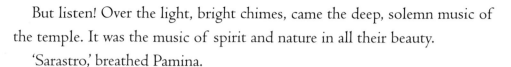

But listen! Over the light, bright chimes, came the deep, solemn music of the temple. It was the music of spirit and nature in all their beauty.

'Sarastro,' breathed Pamina.

Papageno's hands fell from the chimes. Immediately the soldiers stopped dancing and scrabbled about in embarrassment, picking up their weapons, tidying their clothes and smoothing down their ruffled hair. Monostatos advanced threateningly towards Papageno and Pamina, then stopped in his tracks as Sarastro walked in, followed by a band of priests.

'What are we going to tell him?' stuttered Papageno, terrified by the tall, dignified man leading the procession.

'The truth, of course, my friend,' said Pamina, surprised. 'Sarastro always rewards the truth.'

Pamina greeted Sarastro and explained why she had run away.

'You do understand, don't you,' Sarastro said gently, when she had finished, 'that you are here for your own safety?'

Sadly, Pamina bowed her head.

'But I know you have fallen in love, and things must change.'

There was a sudden scuffle as Monostatos thrust his way out of the crowd, shoving and pushing a young man in shackles.

'Tamino!' chorused Pamina and Papageno.

'Indeed it is,' said Monostatos, cockily, 'and what, my Lord Sarastro, is my reward for capturing this villain?'

'A beating,' replied Sarastro, sternly. 'Now release this young man.'

Prince Tamino and Princess Pamina could not take their eyes off each other and, as Monostatos loosened Tamino's chains, the entire group burst out cheering.

Then Sarastro and his priests withdrew into an inner chamber of the temple to decide on an important matter.

'Pamina has fallen in love, my brothers,' Sarastro said. 'And as you know, I want to hand over the work of our brotherhood to her and the man she marries. Tamino is good and honest and we should admit him into our temple. But first we must make sure that he is worthy.'

The others agreed and Sarastro assigned two of them to set tests for Tamino.

The priests found Tamino and Papageno and placed hoods over their heads before leading them to a secret garden. 'If you want to free Pamina,' they said, 'you must be willing to die for the truth.' Tamino agreed readily, but Papageno was not so sure.

The priests removed the hoods from their heads. 'Your ordeal begins now,' they said, leaving the two young men in pitch darkness.

Tamino was full of excitement. He did not care how hard his ordeal would be or what risks he had to take, as long as he could win Pamina's freedom. Suddenly the three ladies from the forest appeared out of nowhere, fluttering around Tamino.

'Forget about this ordeal nonsense,' they wheedled. 'Carry Pamina off home. Think of the power you'll have.'

Tamino held firmly to his promise and tried to stop Papageno frolicking around the women, until at last they disappeared, defeated.

Furious that her assistants had not got their way, the Queen of Night flashed like lightning into Pamina's room. 'This knife must pierce Sarastro's heart,' she thundered, thrusting a dagger at Pamina, which glinted and flashed like a flame. 'Your father gave him the Circle of the Sun before dying. Bring it to me, or you'll never see me again.'

Pamina dropped the dagger in terror as her mother disappeared. 'I won't kill anyone,' she gasped. 'Sarastro uses the Circle to do good things, that's why my father entrusted it to him.'

Monostatos, who had been hiding behind the door, had heard everything. 'Marry me, or I'll tell Sarastro you're going to kill him,' he threatened, seizing his chance. But before Pamina could reply, Sarastro strode in and ordered him away. Monostatos lurched out of the chamber, furious. He was fed up with Sarastro. If he stole the Circle of the Sun and joined the queen, she would give him Pamina.

'Please don't punish my mother,' Pamina begged Sarastro, telling him of the queen's visit.

'Revenge is not the way of our Holy Temple,' Sarastro assured her. 'Your father was our leader before me. Like him, we all believe the way to the True Path is love.'

In the temple garden, the priests congratulated Tamino and Papageno for not being tempted by the three women. Then they placed a delicious meal before them and left, warning them that their trial of silence would start at the sound of trumpets.

As they ate, an old crone came up to Papageno.

'I'm your sweetheart,' she croaked, throwing her arms around him.

Papageno joked back but the crone was deadly serious.

Papageno was alarmed. 'What am I going to do now?' he wondered, looking at Tamino who was helpless with laughter.

'Fat lot of help you are!' grumbled Papageno as the three genies arrived in their flying machine to deliver the magic flute and chimes to their owners, Tamino and Papageno. In the distance, the trumpets sounded.

Tamino put his flute to his lips and played. Pamina, recognising its music, came to find him.

'Tamino!' she called. 'Is all well with you?'

Tamino felt terrible. The last thing he wanted was to be unkind to Pamina but he was bound by his test, so he signalled her to leave.

'Don't you want to see me?' asked Pamina, hurt. Once more, Tamino had to wave her away. Pamina turned to Papageno. 'You said Tamino loved me.'

Papageno hung his head sadly. If he ever found someone to love, he would never send her away. But he and Tamino could only listen in miserable silence as Pamina sang, heartbroken, that her dream of love was gone for ever.

'How sad!' cried Papageno, when she had left. 'I wish I had someone to love, because it's love and only love that makes the world go round!'

Suddenly, the crone was standing behind Papageno. 'I love you, Papageno,' she said. 'Swear you will be true to me for ever.'

'I will,' said Papageno as the test of silence ended. 'I really will.'

The crone tugged at her face and Papageno watched in horror as it came off. Then she stood before him, pretty, feathered and young!

'I'm your Papagena!' she announced. 'I was disguised.'

Papageno held out his arms but a priest stopped him. 'The three-fold pipe has sounded and you must go into the desert for the final test.'

Tamino had no time to explain to Pamina why he had not spoken to her. So Pamina cried all night. At dawn, as the three genies watched the light spreading, they saw her huddled in a corner of the palace garden, planning to kill herself.

'That's not very clever,' they said. 'Come with us to see Tamino.'

Pamina agreed and the three genies transported her to a spot at the foot of two towering mountains. The first was black and spouted a roaring, thundering waterfall. The second was red and spat blazing flames of fire. Tamino was alone. The priests had decided that Papageno was not suitable for their temple and they were right. At this very moment, he was with his Papagena, happily singing 'papa-papa-papa' as they planned their future.

Pamina watched two men lead Tamino towards the roaring waters.

'Tamino!' she called. Tamino, no longer sworn to silence, called back.

'Play the flute, Tamino,' she urged from beside him. 'My father made that flute from the most secret heart of a great oak. Play it and we will be safe.'

So Tamino played the flute and together the two of them walked, unharmed, through the gushing falls and fiery arches. Then, slowly, the ground beneath them began to sink until they found themselves in the most magnificent chamber of the Temple of Isis and Osiris. The air was filled with cheers and blessings.

Sarastro welcomed them. 'Truth has succeeded,' he said. 'Now you are both in charge of the temple and I can rest.'

Monostatos fled for protection to the Queen of Night and her three ladies, who shook with fear and anger.

'Wisdom and light have scared away ignorance and darkness,' Sarastro said, as the evil group faded into shadow.

The prince and princess clasped hands firmly. Together, they were ready to face anything.

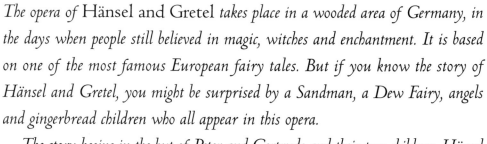

The opera of Hänsel and Gretel *takes place in a wooded area of Germany, in the days when people still believed in magic, witches and enchantment. It is based on one of the most famous European fairy tales. But if you know the story of* Hänsel and Gretel, *you might be surprised by a Sandman, a Dew Fairy, angels and gingerbread children who all appear in this opera.*

The story begins in the hut of Peter and Gertrude and their two children, Hänsel and Gretel. Peter sells brooms for a living but does not earn very much money at all. Brooms are cheap and last a long time so he has no regular customers.

Gertrude tries to help out by selling stockings. But knitting stockings requires time and effort and she has no energy left by the time she comes home after a long day walking up and down the market or calling at people's doors in the hope of selling her wares. So the family often go to bed without enough to eat.

Hänsel and Gretel stay at home, trying to help as much as they can. But sometimes their hard work does not seem worth the effort because there is never a reward at the end of it. Still, they do their best, though sometimes they are distracted by hunger and worn down by the constant toil that goes on day after day.

As the story begins, they are alone at home while their parents have gone off on their daily grind. Hänsel and Gretel are trying to concentrate on their work but they cannot because they feel tired and frustrated. They long for things to be different. If only they could have enough to eat and enjoy a little magic in their lives.

Engelbert Humperdinck was a German composer, teacher and opera critic. He liked to write in a very simple way so his music sounds as if it is based on folk songs. Hänsel and Gretel *is his most famous opera, and it was written in the 1890s.*

Engelbert Humperdinck
1854 ~ 1921

Hänsel and Gretel

ENGELBERT HUMPERDINCK

'I'm hungry,' grumbled Hänsel, adding another twig to a broom. He had been making brooms all day ready for their father to sell in the market tomorrow.

'I know what you mean,' replied Gretel, who was knitting her second stocking.

'I wish Mum and Dad would come home,' continued Hänsel, 'with something nice to eat, for once.'

Gretel placed a jug of milk on the table. 'The neighbour's given us some milk. Mother might make a custard pie.'

'Delicious! I love custard pie.' Hänsel dipped his finger into the cream floating on top of the milk.

'Stop it!' snapped Gretel, though her mouth watered and she felt a huge, twisting feeling inside her stomach as if her hunger had turned into a writhing snake. She heard a distant rumble and looked at Hänsel, clutching his tummy.

'Well, it's been a long time since we ate properly. I can't even remember the taste of bread — forget eggs and butter.'

'Let's think of something cheerful instead of grumbling,' suggested Gretel. Hänsel leapt to his feet and grabbed his sister by the hand. 'Let's dance,' he said, 'anything to take our minds off our tummies. I can't bear to do another stroke of work!'

Gretel was quite happy to stop working and so she took Hänsel's hand and they started prancing around the room. Hänsel was not a very good dancer, but they had a lot of fun pretending to be grand people.

Time passes quickly when you're having fun, and soon the door opened and their mother, Gertrude, stood staring at them.

'Look at you!' scolded Gertrude, furious. 'You've been messing around when

you're supposed to be working! Your father and I slog all day to earn a crust of bread. And here you are, dancing around as if you don't have a thing to worry about. I can't believe it!'

'It was Hänsel ... '

'It was Gretel ... '

'He wanted ... '

'She said I ... '

'Stop trying to blame each other,' snapped Gertrude. She looked in despair at the unfinished stocking and the incomplete broom. And as she flung out her arm to point to them, she knocked the jug of milk off the table.

'Now we've got no supper!' she wailed, looking at the pieces of glass in a pool of milk on the floor. 'Go to the woods. Go on, NOW! And don't come back until the basket is full of strawberries.'

Hänsel and Gretel grabbed the basket and scuttled out very fast. As the door shut behind them, Gertrude slumped down at the table and sobbed herself to sleep. And that was how her husband Peter found her when he waltzed in with a song on his lips. He had sold all his brooms and spent the money on a feast for the family.

'Food!' he beamed, planting a large hamper on the table in front of his wife. 'So much food, you couldn't imagine it!' He swept the napkin off the hamper and let Gertrude feast her eyes on the goodies.

'Hänsel!' he called. 'Gretel! Come and see what's for supper.'

But there was no reply.

'Where are they?' asked Peter.

'Well, they hadn't done their chores, and Gretel put the milk jug on the table and I knocked it over and it was meant to be our supper and the jug broke ... ' Her words turned into a groan as she pointed to the mess on the floor.

'Steady,' said Peter. 'Tell me where they are.'

'I sent them to the woods.'

'Which woods?'

'Ilstenstein Woods.'

Peter slapped his hand to his head. 'My Heavens! That's where the Evil One lives!'

'The Evil One?' wailed Gertrude.

'The Crunch Witch. Every night as the clock strikes midnight, she jumps on her broom and flies out through her chimney, high into the sky and all the way to who knows where, to dance until dawn with other evil creatures. Oven-baked children are her favourite food.'

'Dear God, don't let the witch get my children,' prayed Gertrude. She ran out of the hut towards Ilstenstein Woods, with Peter close behind.

In the woods, the children's basket was filled to the top with strawberries. Gretel sank down on a bed of eglantine flowers and picked some to make a garland for her mother. Somewhere above, a cuckoo called.

'You know what cuckoos do, don't you?' said Gretel. 'They eat what's not theirs.' She popped a strawberry into her mouth.

'Cuc-koo,' said Hänsel grabbing a couple, 'me too.'

'Oi, that's not fair. You had two!' Gretel lunged for the basket and shoved a fistful of strawberries into her mouth.

'Huh! You greedy cuckoo, taking what's not yours. I'll teach you!'

Hänsel put the basket to his mouth and tipped it. Gretel saw the strawberries disappear.

'Oh no, Hänsel! What are we going to do now? Mother will be furious if we go back without them. We have to pick some more.'

'But I can't see properly,' said Hänsel, looking wildly around. 'It's getting dark, we'll never find our way.'

The sun was setting and the shadows grew all around them, forming into strange shapes. Everything looked so different, neither Hänsel nor Gretel could remember the way home.

'I can see someone,' whispered Gretel. 'I'm scared.'

'Don't be silly.' Hänsel was alarmed. 'There's no one here except us – and a few birds.'

'Is anyone here?' Gretel called in a shaky voice.

'Here. Here. Here,' came the echo.

All around them the mist came down and settled between the trees like a huge curtain. And the wind moaned and groaned like a wounded monster.

'Help,' yelled Hänsel and Gretel, clinging to each other. 'Help! Someone please help!'

'Help,' mocked the echo and the cuckoo called too – one last time. Her friendly voice seemed to taunt them now, like the echo.

'Look, Hänsel,' Gretel nudged her brother. The mist had cleared in one corner of the glade and there, almost completely blending into the murky, forest twilight, stood a small grey manikin with a heavy bag slung over his shoulder.

'The Sandman,' they thought, as he smiled drowsily and flung some slumber-dust at them. It settled into their eyes, making their lids heavy. Without another word, they sank to their knees, said their bedtime prayers and fell fast asleep.

As they rested, a dazzling column of light shone through the mist and seven pairs of angels came slowly down. They arranged themselves around Hänsel and Gretel and spread out their wings to keep them safe through the night.

At dawn, the Dew Fairy flicked dew from a bluebell and it glistened like jewels on the flowers and foliage. Some dewdrops fell on Hänsel and Gretel, too, and they opened their eyes.

'Wake up, Hänsel,' said Gretel, as her brother rolled over to go back to sleep. 'It's morning.'

Hänsel sat up and rubbed his eyes. 'I had a strange dream last night,' he recalled. 'There were all these angels and' ... 'they came down and guarded us,' finished Gretel, bright-eyed.

Hänsel's mouth fell open. 'You had the same dream!'

As they stared at each other, the mist rose and there in front of them was a house. And what a house it was! Surely, surely it had been sent to them by the angels! It was moulded in cake, covered in chocolate cream and decorated with thin, crackly icing.

'Let's have some,' shouted Hänsel.

'You can't just stuff yourself,' scolded Gretel. 'It belongs to someone.'

'Yes, us!' argued Hänsel. 'The angels gave it to us!'

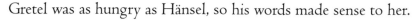

Gretel was as hungry as Hänsel, so his words made sense to her.

Quietly, they crept up to the house and sank their hands into its walls. Thick slabs of plum cake filled their palms.

'Nibble, nibble, mousekin, who's nibbling at my housekin?' came a murmuring sound.

Hänsel dropped the cake he was eating. Gretel stood still. 'Did you hear someone?'

Hänsel listened. 'It's the wind,' he mumbled.

'The wind, of course,' agreed Gretel, wanting to believe they were safe and free to eat as much as they liked.

The two of them played and joked as they ate. They were having so much fun that they did not notice the Crunch Witch sneak up behind them and slip a noose around Hänsel's neck.

'Nibble, nibble, mousekin, who's nibbling at my housekin?' she repeated. Gretel laughed cheekily: 'Don't be so mean, Mr Wind, let us eat in peace.'

A screeching cackle filled the air. Hänsel yelled and struggled as he realised he was trapped. Gretel turned to see a woman dressed all in black. She had a stick in her hand and she was holding the noose. Her hair was wild and stuck out from beneath her hat, and her gown swirled like a thundercloud as she spoke in a voice that chilled Gretel's bones.

'How nice of you to come and see me. I love little children. Come in, come in, and see the goodies I have for you.'

'Let go. Who are you?' yelled Hänsel, struggling.

'I'm Rosine Finelips,' the witch crooned, pulling him nearer. 'Come into my house and stop being so suspicious.'

'Never!' Hänsel yanked himself away, fighting the rope.

'Leave my brother alone!' shouted Gretel.

'I'm only going to feed him up, put some flesh on those bones – and if he's good, he'll have a surprise.' She flicked her hair and licked her lips.

'I don't trust you,' said Hänsel, slipping free. 'Come on, Gretel, run.'

But the witch acted fast. She snatched an elder wand from her belt and raised it high, chanting a magic spell. The tip of the wand glowed and glimmered like a smouldering ember; Hänsel and Gretel stood hypnotised, unable to tear their gaze from it. The witch led Hänsel to a cage in the courtyard, opened the door and pushed him in. Gretel stood where she was, bound still by the spell. The witch pinched Hänsel hard on his arm.

'Ouch!' he yelped. 'Don't!'

The witch cackled and pinched his thigh. Hänsel squealed.

'What do you think you're doing?' demanded Gretel.

'Feeling if he's fat enough, of course.'

'Fat enough for what?' demanded Gretel.

'To eat, naturally. Boys are my favourite meal. So succulent. Girls are fine – but boys are especially delicious. Boy soup and boy stew are terribly nutritious.'

'That's disgusting,' said Gretel, still unable to move. The witch pointed a menacing finger at her and went inside to build a fire in the hot, grimy stove that smoked and grunted in the corner of her kitchen. 'I've got to bake my gingerbread,' she chuckled. 'It's almost mid-morning. Time for a meal.'

'She's really horrible,' said Gretel, standing rigid as a pole.

Hänsel put his finger to his lips, 'Shhh. Stop shouting. She'll hear you. Now listen, Gretel, just do everything she says and don't worry about me. Shush now. She's coming back.'

The witch appeared in the doorway, carrying a basket of almonds and raisins. She looked at Gretel, making sure she was quite still, then crouched down beside Hänsel's cage and tried to push some nuts into his mouth. Hänsel pretended to be asleep.

'Boys,' grinned the Crunch Witch. 'They'll sleep through anything.'

She wandered over to Gretel, waving an elder stick and chanting a freeing spell. Suddenly, Gretel could move.

'Go into the house,' the witch commanded, 'and lay the table.' Then excitedly, she jumped on to her broom and whizzed around the candy house singing a ditty:

> So hop, hop, hop, gallop, lop, lop
> My broomstick horse move without force

At crack of dawn you'll see me gone
Here, there and everywhere!

As you can imagine, the exercise made the Crunch Witch hungry. But she decided to check on Hänsel first, to see just how much she would have to fatten him before he was ready for the oven.

'Show me your finger,' she commanded. Hänsel found he could move when the witch asked him to. Cunningly, he stuck out an old chicken bone he had found in the cage.

'Ooh! Still skin and bones,' said the witch. 'Oi. Girl! Bring me some more almonds and raisins.'

Gretel appeared with a basket of almonds and raisins and the witch crammed them into Hänsel's mouth. Behind her, Gretel held up the elder stick, waving it as the witch had done, and muttered the spell to free Hänsel.

The Crunch Witch wheeled round. 'What did you say?'

'Nothing,' said Gretel, hiding the stick behind her.

The witch forced a handful of raisins into Gretel's mouth. 'That should shut you up.'

'Be careful,' Hänsel mouthed to his sister, behind the witch's back. 'She's planning to eat you.'

'See if the gingerbread's done,' screeched the Crunch Witch.

'I don't know how,' faked Gretel.

'Bend over and put your head into the oven until you can get a good look.'

'I don't know what you mean.'

'Just do as I say. It's easy.' The witch said impatiently to Gretel. Hänsel crept quietly out of his cage.

'If you're so good at it, show me,' said Gretel, cheekily, skipping into the kitchen to keep the witch from seeing Hänsel.

The witch followed her in and stomped over to the oven. She lowered herself and leaned deep into its enormous belly, reaching for the gingerbread. Hänsel and Gretel put their hands on her bottom and shoved with all their

might, until finally, with a whoosh, she slid right in. Then they banged the door shut.

'Hurrah!' they sang. 'The witch is dead!'

As they waltzed around the room, they could hear a sputter, which turned into a crackle and a rattle. Finally with an enormous BOOM! the oven exploded. Hänsel and Gretel were knocked to the ground. When they came to their senses, they saw a band of children, partly covered in chunks of crumbling gingerbread. Their eyes were shut and they could not move.

'Touch us,' they begged, 'so that we can open our eyes and see.' Cautiously, Gretel inched forward and touched them, one by one. But though they opened their eyes, they still could not move.

Hänsel reached for the elder stick and in a loud, clear voice, he chanted the freeing spell. The next moment, the children were laughing and cheering, clapping and dancing, thrilled to be alive. Their voices rang around the forest and above, far and wide and deep inside and all the way to where Peter and Gertrude were still desperately searching for their children.

They hurried to follow the sound and soon entered the glade where the children were celebrating their freedom. The whole family threw themselves into each other's arms, asking questions, saying they were sorry and checking everyone was safe. Goodness knows how long they would have gone on this way if the rest of the children hadn't struggled out with a gigantic loaf of bread, which they had dragged from the exploded oven. And do you know, there was something about that loaf that reminded everyone of the Crunch Witch?

Richard Wagner
1813 – 1883

The story of The Flying Dutchman *is set in the eighteenth century in a fishing village in Norway.*

It is based on an old legend famous all over Scandinavia, Germany and Austria. According to the legend, hundreds of years ago a Dutch sea captain was travelling far away from Europe, near the Cape of Good Hope in Africa, when his ship ran into a terrible storm. The captain struggled long and hard to save his ship but his efforts proved useless. Tired and hopeless and by now very frightened, he could think of only one way to save his ship, The Dutchman, and his crew.

He made a pact with the Devil: in return for surviving the storm, he and his crew would agree to live for ever by giving their souls to the Devil. But the pact, made in fear and haste, proved far worse than death. The captain and crew sailed the seas for centuries, on The Dutchman, exhausted and melancholy, with only one hope of salvation. The captain had to find a woman who would be faithful to him in spite of his terrible past. If he did, the curse would be lifted. To accomplish this, he was allowed off the boat on to land for a single day and night every seven years. But so far, time after time after time, the captain returned to the ship, alone and world-weary, after another wasted night ashore. Could a woman exist who had the courage and compassion to help the cursed captain by going with him to his ghostly vessel?

As the opera begins, Daland, another captain, is fighting to save his ship and crew in a storm off the coast of Norway. He is forced to drop anchor on a strange beach. This is also the night when the Dutch captain is allowed ashore. And their paths are destined to cross.

Richard Wagner was born in Germany, and his works are unusual as he was a poet as well as a composer, and so wrote both the words and the music. He produced epic operas, the most famous of which is the Ring Cycle, *four great operas based on Norse legends.*

The Flying Dutchman

RICHARD WAGNER

Captain Daland was downhearted. A storm had forced his ship, *The Norwegian*, off course just when he was about to bring it home to Sandwike, in Norway, after months of travelling away at sea. Well, at least the worst was over now and they were safely anchored, although Daland had never before seen this deserted stretch of coast with its ragged cliffs looming above. It was nearly dawn as he stepped ashore and climbed to the top of a cliff to work out their exact location. They were seven miles from home – closer than he had hoped.

Relieved, he returned to his ship, praised his crew for their hard work and sent them to rest, planning to keep watch. But his young steersman offered to stay instead and Daland went gratefully down to his cabin.

Up on deck, the steersman, who had also worked hard most of the night, kept sleep at bay by singing a song which sailors sing about the loved ones they have left behind. But, as you know, when sleep is determined to come, it gets the better of you, and so the steersman fell asleep.

As soon as his eyes closed, a silent mass began to emerge from the heavy sea mist.

An eerie glow lit the hulk of a ship. Its sails were as red as blood, billowing against tall black masts. The ship dropped anchor and a violent crash echoed in the night. The steersman awoke with a start but saw nothing. Tired from the day's excitement, he fell asleep again.

Silent as a dream, the ship drew close to *The Norwegian* and a tall man, dressed in old-fashioned clothes, stepped soundlessly ashore. There was an air of long ago about him, and misery and anger clung to him like skin, as well they might.

Many years ago — maybe even a hundred or more — this man had run into a terrible storm on the African coast. And he had been so scared for the safety of his ship that he had made a pact with the Devil: in return for survival he would sail the seas for evermore in Satan's grip, unable to die. Oh, he had tried hard enough to end his life after coming to his senses and realising what a hard bargain the Devil had driven. He challenged the cruellest pirates to battle but they backed away. He drove his ship aground on rocks but it only floated free again. So the captain wandered on, restless and tormented, praying, longing, begging for the eternal peace that only death would bring.

Every seven years, though, he could bring his boat to harbour and step on to solid land. If at this time he found a woman to love him faithfully, he would gain forgiveness and peace.

Daland's stern voice woke the steersman. 'What kind of watch do you call this? That could be a pirate vessel out there.'

Startled, the steersman opened his eyes and saw the mysterious ship. 'Who are you?' he called. But there was no answer. Then Daland spotted the mysterious man ashore.

'Hello!' he called, leaning over in his direction. 'Where are you from?'

'A long way away,' replied the man. 'Seeking refuge from the storm.'

Daland made his way down to him. 'Tell me who you are.'

'I'm the captain of that ship.' He pointed a sombre finger at his craft. 'It is called *The Dutchman*.'

'I'm Daland. We're sheltering from the storm, too. Any damage?'

The captain shook his head. 'I've travelled for years. I'm under a curse. Nothing damages my ship — or me. I wander on in search of home and rest. But do I find it? Never! I'm condemned to eternal restlessness.'

Daland was baffled by the captain's odd speech. He felt very sorry for him.

'Take me home and I'll give you gold and jewels — as many as you want,' offered the Dutch captain, his eyes full of longing.

'I'm not quite sure what to make of your story,' replied Daland, 'but I'm willing to help. Tell me about your cargo.'

'Come and see for yourself. Pearls, rubies, diamonds, gold – take them.'

'In return for what?' Daland asked, even more puzzled.

'For one night in your home. And there's more in the hold. It's no use to me. I have no wife to share it with. Just take me into your home.'

'I must admit, I'm confused,' replied Daland who could not believe he was being offered all this wealth for something he would have done anyway.

'Do you have a daughter?' the captain asked.

Daland nodded. 'Senta, she's delightful.'

'Let me marry her.'

Daland was both surprised and pleased. Every father wants to find his daughter a rich and generous husband and this strange, sad man definitely had both qualities.

'Let me marry your daughter and I'll give you everything I have.'

'Well,' replied Daland. 'Come and meet her. She's lovely – and she looks after me well.'

'Then she will be faithful to me,' murmured the Dutch captain. 'When can I meet her?'

Daland believed that the captain was a good man who had suffered enough and deserved better luck from now on. The south wind was favourable to their journey and they set sail immediately so that the captain could meet Senta.

At home in Sandwike, Senta and her friends sat spinning. But while they sang to make their work easier, Senta brooded. Her mind was on a different song – the ballad of *The Flying Dutchman*. It told a sad, haunting story and Senta's eyes often wandered from her work to the picture of the Flying Dutchman that hung on the wall.

A strange man in old-fashioned clothes looked back at Senta with sorrowful and tormented eyes.

'You behave as if you know him,' complained her nurse Mary.

'I know all about him,' replied Senta. 'His story is heartbreaking. Can you imagine drifting on the sea, lonely and tired, for ever?'

The others fell silent as Senta spoke and, almost as if in a dream, she began to sing the ballad of *The Flying Dutchman*. When she had finished, she wiped the tears from her eyes.

'Well, I hope he'll find a faithful wife one day,' said Mary, shivering a little. 'I'll pray for him.'

Senta jumped to her feet, cheeks flushed. 'I know!' she exclaimed. 'I'll be the one. I'll marry him and be faithful to him and redeem him from the curse.'

'You can't!' protested Erik, the young hunter, as he stalked in to tell her that Daland was back. 'You promised to marry me.'

'My father's here?' Senta dashed for the door, followed by the girls. 'Hang on!' yelled Mary. 'Don't forget the sailors' feast. We have to prepare the food, remember?'

The girls returned to the house, pretending to moan and complain. But the sailors were mostly their husbands and sweethearts and they did not really mind preparing the feast.

As the women put away their wool, Daland came in. Beside him, gazing at Senta with tormented eyes, was the Dutch captain. Senta stared back, hypnotised.

'You're so fascinated with our guest you haven't greeted your father,' joked Daland. 'And it's just as well.' His voice became gentle. 'Senta, my child, I have promised the captain here that you will marry him.'

Then, leaving them to discuss the matter, he excused himself to prepare for the sailors' feast.

'You probably don't like your father's choice,' murmured the Dutchman when the captain had gone.

'I do, because I've decided to save your soul,' thought Senta, but aloud she said, 'My father has asked me to marry you, and I'll obey.'

'Are you sure?' persisted the captain. 'Life with me will not be easy. There are terrible things in store. You must be absolutely certain you can stay faithful in spite of them – otherwise, the result will be unbearable.'

'Don't worry,' Senta assured him. 'I have made up my mind to save you and nothing will make me change it.'

45

Senta could hear centuries of torment in the Dutch captain's sigh of relief. 'Thank you,' he breathed, 'you'll rescue me from the powers of darkness. I'll rest at last. You can't know what this means.'

'But I do,' insisted Senta.

'What have you decided, my child?' inquired Daland, returning to the room. 'Have you consented to marry the captain?'

'She has,' replied the Dutch captain. 'So a pure-hearted girl will defeat the Devil. Senta will be my salvation.'

Daland was delighted with the decision and promised to announce the news at the feast.

That night, the sea was calm. Aboard *The Norwegian*, the sailors sang and danced, watching the girls come out of Daland's house laden with food and drink for the feast.

'Here,' they yelled. 'Bring it over!'

'It's not for you,' teased the girls. 'It's for our guests aboard the Dutch vessel.' The strange ship stood dark and moody against the open sky.

'Look,' joked the Norwegians. 'No sign of life. Everyone's asleep.'

The girls moved towards the ship and called out, offering their freshly baked bread and cool wine. But there was no answer. Silence hung heavy and still, making the girls back away in fear.

'It's like the legend of *The Flying Dutchman*,' muttered the sailors. 'It's a ghost ship for sure. It's even called *The Dutchman*.'

As they discussed the ship and its ghostly crew, a dark cloud descended over *The Dutchman*. The waters, tranquil everywhere else, began to bubble and froth around her hull and her sails were battered back and forth by a gale. Then all at once, a blue flame reared up on deck and slowly the shadowy figures of the crew came to life and moved about in the distance, singing as they went about their work. They sang about their haunted captain who after every seven years returned to his ship and its crew, without a wife, doomed to the Devil's care.

The sailors and the girls listened, petrified, to the ominous song. They were right. This was the unearthly craft of the legend! The song of the grisly crew sent shivers down the spines of the Norwegian lads and lasses. They sang loudly, hoping to drown it out. But the Dutch crew just sang louder. At last, the Norwegian sailors stopped singing and made the sign of the cross to protect themselves. The Dutch crew laughed and jeered as they watched. But then, all at once, everything grew still and silent aboard *The Dutchman*. Darkness descended, the wind fell and the sky cleared.

The door of Daland's cottage opened and Senta walked towards *The Dutchman*.

'You are mad!' yelled Erik, running after her. 'You can't go there.'

'Leave me alone, Erik,' begged Senta. 'I can't explain – but I know I have to save the Dutch captain.'

'Heaven help you,' cried Erik. 'You've been bewitched by a dark power. You promised to marry me. How can you break your word?'

'Did I promise?' Senta looked blank as she continued to walk away.

'How could you forget?' They neared *The Dutchman*. Erik spoke urgently. 'It was a sunny day in the middle of summer. Your father was just setting out to sea. He asked me to look after you while he was away. Did I imagine that day?'

Senta faltered as she heard Erik's words.

'You've betrayed me!' The words resounded in the air like a cannon blast. Senta turned to see the captain standing behind her. 'I'm doomed for ever!'

Erik jumped back, terrified, as the voice continued. 'Goodbye, Senta. I forgive you.'

'You poor man! Don't go!' pleaded Senta, as the captain walked away. 'I haven't betrayed you.'

'I can bring you nothing but misery,' the captain declared. 'What sort of life would you have with me? You were right to break your word, Senta.'

'But I didn't!' Senta protested, trying to break free of Erik's grasp. 'Prepare to sail!' the captain commanded his crew. 'We're condemned to roam the seas until the end of the world.'

'If you won't believe me,' Senta challenged, 'come ashore and take me with you.'

'Don't make fun of me, Senta,' the captain begged. 'I've accepted my fate. I'm happy that you don't have to share my misery.'

'Senta, you're in that Devil's power,' Erik gasped. 'Let me save you. Help! Someone rescue Senta.'

'You are safe, Senta,' the captain continued, 'because I protected you from the Devil. You made him no promise, or you, too, would be eternally damned. You could not help me, Senta, but I saved you from Satan. You are free of me – you might as well know that I am the dreaded Flying Dutchman.'

Senta wrenched herself free from Erik and ran towards him. 'I've known all along,' she announced. But the Dutch captain didn't hear her as he strode purposefully towards his ship.

By now, some sailors from *The Norwegian* had come down in response to Erik's calls and they were joined by the girls. The Dutch captain leapt on to his boat. Senta tried to follow but the others held her down.

With a strong tug, Senta broke free again, raced to the edge of the cliff and hurled herself over. Her words rent the air, loud and clear as a bell: 'I will free you from the curse and prove my loyalty.'

As the others watched, *The Dutchman* began to tilt and sway, then spinning full circle, it sank swiftly into a whirlpool. And in the orange glow of the rising sun, they saw the figures of Senta and the Flying Dutchman float merrily upwards into the sky.

Senta had been faithful to the Flying Dutchman and freed him from the Devil's clutches. At last, he would rest in eternal peace. Senta had fulfilled her promise and she would be his companion for evermore.

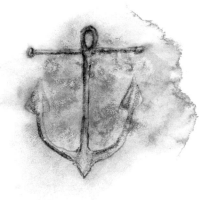

Tisbe

Clorinda

La Cenerentola

GIOACCHINO ROSSINI

Angelina ~
known to all as
"Cenerentola"

Don Magnifico ~
a Baron ~
Father to Clorinda
and Tisbe ~
Step-father to
Cenerentola

Alidoro ~
a philosopher and
the prince's tutor

Don Ramiro ~
Prince of Salerno
(disguised as his valet)

Dandini ~
Royal Valet
(disguised as the prince)

The story of La Cenerentola *is set in the eighteenth century in Salerno, Italy. It is one of the most famous fairy tales ever, which perhaps you know as* Cinderella. *But in this opera, you'll find 'Cinderella' has a step-father rather than a step-mother and bracelets rather than glass slippers.*

Cenerentola lived with her step-father, Don Magnifico, and his two daughters, Clorinda and Tisbe, in the castle Montefiasco. After Cenerentola's mother died, she longed to be a good daughter to Don Magnifico. Although he was a baron, Don Magnifico had squandered all his money and he could not afford a servant, so it was useful to have Cenerentola to fetch and carry. She cooked and cleaned willingly, hoping that Don Magnifico and his daughters would treat her as family, but she could never please them.

Don Magnifico wanted a wealthy husband for each of his two daughters so that he could live a life of luxury. He lavished fine clothes on Clorinda and Tisbe and took them to grand parties to catch rich husbands. Meanwhile Cenerentola was dressed shabbily and waited on them hand and foot, but she did not lose spirit. She was sure she would marry a nice young man one day. To cheer herself up — and also to annoy her sisters — she sang a song about a prince who, given the choice of three sisters, saw through the beauty and finery of the older two and chose the third for her kindness.

But a surprise was waiting around the corner for Cenerentola . . .

The king of the country had died, ruling that his son should marry before being crowned. Prince Ramiro had no idea where to look for a suitable bride. Alidoro, his wise tutor and adviser, came to his aid. He told Ramiro and his assistant, Dandini, to swap places while he, Alidoro, would dress as a beggar and provide his own report. That way, Ramiro could judge from a distance who would make him a suitable bride.

Gioacchino Rossini was born in Italy, the son of musical parents. As a boy he sang in the opera at Bologna, but he grew up to be famous for his comic operas and delicious pasta recipes!

Gioacchino
Rossini
1792 ~ 1868

La Cenerentola

GIOACCHINO ROSSINI

Clorinda and Tisbe preened themselves in front of a large mirror. Did these flowers make them look pretty? Did they look smart in that hat? Ah, but weren't they both beautiful?

'A lonely prince searched for a bride,' sang their young step-sister Cenerentola, prodding the logs into flame, as she made the coffee. 'But who of three sisters could he choose? He left the pretty one and he left the smart one, he wanted the one who was kind.'

'Shut up, Cenerentola,' yelled Clorinda.

'Yes, shut up,' echoed Tisbe, as a loud knock sounded on the door. 'See who's there.'

Still humming, Cenerentola obeyed. An old man stood outside looking tired, hungry and very cold.

'Come in,' said Cenerentola, her heart melting. 'I'll get you some coffee.'

'No, you won't!' screeched Clorinda.

'It's our coffee,' added Tisbe.

Cenerentola poured extra coffee into the cup and handed it to the beggar. It was as if she had broken the law! Clorinda and Tisbe fell on her, kicking and slapping. The beggar, who was really Alidoro, advisor to Prince Ramiro, could not believe his eyes.

'Stop it!' he commanded sharply, just as a stream of grandly dressed people trooped in.

'We're here to tell Don Magnifico and his daughters that Prince Ramiro is coming to invite you to his country home where he will choose a bride.'

'How kind,' cooed Clorinda and Tisbe, pretending to be shy. 'How exciting.'
But when the courtiers left, it was a different story. Their smiles turned to

scowls and their voices turned shrill as they yelled instructions at Cenerentola. 'Fetch this, carry that, lace my shoes, comb my hair, mend this, sew that and hurry with the other.'

'That's not fair,' grumbled Cenerentola. 'What about me? I'm invited too. Besides, I'm not a slave. Why should I do all the fetching and carrying?'

But Clorinda and Tisbe would not listen. They were too busy arguing and bossing her about.

And the sound of their quarrelling awakened their father who stumbled in, furious, still in his pyjamas.

Clorinda and Tisbe giggled. They knew Don Magnifico would stop being angry the moment he heard what the noise was about.

'Stop laughing and listen to my dream,' he insisted. 'I saw this donkey and suddenly it grew feathers and wings and soared up to the steeple. The bells chimed out marvellously and then ... ' He stopped, scowling. 'And then, you woke me up. The bells in my dream mean joy in my home,' he went on, brightening up. 'The feathers stand for you — my daughters; the flying means great honour. And I expect I am that fabulous donkey. So the dream means my daughters will be queens and I'll have royal grandchildren.'

'Well, you just might be right,' twittered Clorinda and Tisbe, telling him about Ramiro's invitation. 'The prince is coming to fetch us to his country palace.'

Don Magnifico sat down with a thump. 'This could change everything,' he said, looking around at the collapsing walls. 'I could restore this castle and start living well again. Now go on! Make the best of yourselves!' Then he looked down at his own clothes and hurriedly rushed out after his daughters to get dressed.

A few moments later, when Prince Ramiro walked into the room, disguised as his own assistant, Dandini, he found the room empty. Ramiro did not want to get married at all. But his father, the king, had died suddenly, insisting that Ramiro could not be king unless he married.

'There was a lonely prince ...' trilled Cenerentola. She sailed into the room and came face to face with Ramiro. Goodness! Had her song come true? 'My heart's thumping!' she gasped.

'Why?' demanded Ramiro. 'Am I a demon?'

'No ... but I wasn't expecting to find anyone here. Who are you?'

'I'm Dandini, Prince Ramiro's assistant,' fibbed Ramiro, thinking how beautiful she was. 'I've come to fetch Don Magnifico's daughters. Are you one of them?'

'Yes, I am,' stuttered Cenerentola. 'Well, actually, I'm not. That is, I'm sort of ... oh, I can't explain.'

'Cenerentola!' screeched Clorinda and Tisbe from upstairs.

'I'm coming!' replied Cenerentola, sorry to leave the young man. Why was such a pretty, delicate girl dressed so shabbily wondered Ramiro, making up his mind to find out. Any moment now his assistant, Dandini, would come in disguised as the prince, and Ramiro could stand back to watch what everyone was really like. Then he would learn about the girl.

And here came Dandini, followed by the courtiers. And there, the baron and his daughters stood, ready to greet them. Clorinda and Tisbe were so busy staring at the prince, who was really Dandini, that they did not even spot Alidoro, who had returned in the prince's retinue.

'Oh, Your Highness!' Dandini whispered to the prince. 'What a job you've given me! I've met dozens of women but not one right for you.'

'Welcome, Your Highness!' smarmed Clorinda, bowing low to Dandini.

'It is so kind of you to honour us,' flattered Tisbe, smiling sweetly.

'So good of you,' added Don Magnifico.

'Do people always behave like this with royalty?' Dandini whispered to Ramiro, between lavish comments to Don Magnifico and his daughters. But Ramiro was still thinking of Cenerentola.

'Where is she?' he wondered. 'Why isn't she coming back?'

Dandini turned back to Don Magnifico and his daughters. 'My courtiers will accompany you to my country residence and I will meet you there.'

Ramiro was disappointed. He had discovered nothing about Cenerentola. Before joining the others, he took a last hopeful look inside the house. And there, framed in the doorway, was Cenerentola. Don Magnifico saw her too.

'Fetch my cloak and walking stick!' he ordered.

'Please let me come to the ball,' begged Cenerentola, handing him his cane.

'Out of my sight, girl!' barked Don Magnifico.

Ramiro stood rooted to the spot in anger.

'Just for an hour,' Cenerentola pleaded. Don Magnifico raised his stick.

'Stop!' said Ramiro, gripping the baron's hand, hard.

'I apologise for this kitchen maid,' said Don Magnifico, bowing to Dandini.

'Is she really a kitchen maid?' inquired Ramiro, suspiciously.

'She is.'

'That's what you'd like me to be,' muttered Cenerentola.

Don Magnifico rounded on her. 'Get out of here. You cheeky little … '

'Why must I always be stuck here cooking and cleaning?' objected Cenerentola. 'Please let me come!' She laid her hand on her step-father's arm. Roughly, Don Magnifico shook it off and followed Dandini.

'One moment,' said Alidoro, who had been quietly watching. 'According to my list you have three daughters. The prince is entitled to meet all three.'

Don Magnifico shifted uneasily. 'The third one died,' he blurted out.

'That's not what my register says,' Alidoro challenged.

'I'm not dead!' spluttered Cenerentola, shocked, but Don Magnifico was back beside her, coughing loudly to drown her words.

'You soon will be!' he hissed menacingly, as the royal party swept out.

Alidoro waited until everyone had gone. Then he spoke comfortingly to Cenerentola. 'Get a smile on your face, daughter, and stop worrying.' Cenerentola smiled through her tears. 'It's nice to be called daughter,' she murmured. 'My step-father would rather die than call me that.'

'That's his loss,' said Alidoro gently. 'Now don't worry about a thing.'

Back in the palace everyone was having fun except Ramiro. He could not get Cenerentola out of his mind. Clorinda and Tisbe bowed and scraped to Dandini, while Don Magnifico showed off his great knowledge of wine.

'Go and inspect the cellar,' said Dandini, hoping to get rid of him. 'If you're still standing after thirteen glasses, you can be Royal Wine Master.'

Don Magnifico was jubilant. Wine Master to the palace! That would put an end to his money problems. So, down he went into the cellar to try his luck. At last Ramiro managed to get a quiet moment with Dandini.

'What are they like?' he asked. 'Alidoro favours the youngest.'

'Oh, Alidoro,' scoffed Dandini, who had secretly fallen in love with Cenerentola himself. 'What does he know?'

Clorinda and Tisbe were just about to claim Dandini's attention again when they noticed he was staring at someone else. Like all the others in the room, he was looking at the door.

As the party watched, a veiled woman entered the room accompanied by Alidoro. Ramiro's heart leapt. Clorinda and Tisbe looked cross and jealous. The courtiers moved forward, full of curiosity. If everyone was already so enchanted by this stranger, how would they react when she removed her veil?

'I don't want wealth and glory,' said the veiled woman, in a musical voice. 'I want my husband's respect and kindness.'

Ramiro thought he knew the voice. It was the girl from Don Magnifico's castle. Dandini floated forward, dazed, begging the stranger to remove her veil. Clorinda and Tisbe hissed spitefully to each other that she would be nowhere near as lovely as either of them. The mysterious woman removed her veil and looked shyly at Ramiro. Instantly, he knew her. Alidoro chuckled to himself, satisfied. His job was done. Ramiro had found a perfect bride.

'Dinner is served,' announced Don Magnifico, bustling in, but the smug grin died on his lips. He stared at Cenerentola. Alidoro watched as he rushed over to his daughters and they whispered together in panic. Could this be Cenerentola? Surely not? Cenerentola did not own a single decent gown. Besides, she was scruffy and hadn't the grace to carry off a gown like this.

All through dinner, the courtiers whispered and wondered about the mysterious visitor.

'I wonder who she is?'

'Ramiro can't take his eyes off her!'

'Neither can Dandini! He's forgetting he's only prince for one night!'

At last the meal was over and Ramiro slipped out on to the balcony to think quietly on his own. He had only been there a moment when Cenerentola came

in followed by Dandini. Swiftly, Ramiro hid behind a pillar. He had to know for sure if Cenerentola loved him, Ramiro, and not just the title of Prince.

Dandini fell to his knees before Cenerentola. 'I love you,' he announced.

'Don't say that!' retorted Cenerentola, stepping back.

'Why?' Dandini looked hurt and surprised.

'I'm sorry,' relented Cenerentola, 'but I love your assistant.'

Ramiro stepped out from behind the pillar. 'Don't you want to marry a rich prince?' he asked.

'No,' replied Cenerentola, firmly. 'I'd prefer a kind man who loves me.'

'Then you'll marry me?'

Cenerentola handed Ramiro a bracelet. 'You will recognise me by the twin to this bracelet. If you still want me when you find me, I'll marry you.'

The next moment she was gone, leaving Ramiro to puzzle over her words. Dandini slipped back into the reception hall.

'Have you chosen one of my daughters?' asked the baron, ambling over.

'What do you expect from your daughter's husband?' asked Dandini.

'Well,' hedged Don Magnifico, 'just the usual things. A palace for a home, horse-drawn carriages, riches and jewels, fabulous delicacies to eat … you know the sort of thing.'

'I have none of those things,' confessed Dandini. He knew the baron would soon discover who he was, so he decided to tell him that he was not Prince Ramiro at all, but his assistant in disguise. Well, Don Magnifico was furious!

'Ramiro has made a fool of me,' he spluttered. 'I demand an explanation. I am a baron.'

'I'll give you a baron,' snapped Dandini, snatching up a stick and waving it at Don Magnifico.

'He's crazy enough to use that,' thought the baron. And he scurried off home, herding Clorinda and Tisbe before him, all of them furious with the strange guest who looked so much like Cenerentola.

When they got home, Cenerentola was sitting by the fire. Clorinda and Tisbe glared at her. Could she really, truly be the mysterious visitor?

'Why are you staring at me?' Cenerentola demanded.

'We met a witch,' the baron snarled. 'She looks exactly like you.'

'Ooh!' rasped Clorinda between gritted teeth. 'I'm so-oo furious.' Outside, a storm brewed up. Thunder roared and lightning flashed. Inside, the baron and his daughters raged at Cenerentola.

'Why are you so angry?' she asked but they just scolded and criticised.

'If only the storm would drown Dandini!' seethed the baron, as the wind howled outside.

The door opened and Dandini walked in, as if he'd heard his name spoken. 'The prince's coach has broken down,' he said. 'We need shelter.'

Ramiro stepped forward. 'I'm sorry about the deception,' he began but Don Magnifico interrupted him. If the prince is here, he thought, surely it is because he wants to marry Clorinda or Tisbe. So he made Ramiro welcome.

'Cenerentola!' he yelled. 'Bring in the best chair for the prince.' Cenerentola came in and placed the chair beside Dandini.

'That's the prince, you idiot,' jeered Don Magnifico, pointing to Ramiro.

Cenerentola froze. 'It can't be!' she thought, startled. 'That's his assistant.'

'Go back to the kitchen!' commanded the baron seeing Ramiro's look.

'Let me see your hands,' said Ramiro, calling her back.

Cenerentola did as he asked. And there, on her wrist, was the other bracelet.

'You have no manners,' Clorinda chided Cenerentola.

'What you need is a beating,' fumed Tisbe.

'One more word,' warned Ramiro, 'and you will be punished. This is my future bride.'

Don Magnifico was astounded. How could the prince choose a kitchen-maid above his daughters?

'For my sake, Your Highness,' Cenerentola said, 'please forgive them.'

But Prince Ramiro was not at all sure. 'Look at them,' he exclaimed. 'They're still calling you names.'

Still, Cenerentola insisted and at last she won over Don Magnifico, Clorinda and Tisbe with her kind words. To make Cenerentola happy, Ramiro forgave them. Then they all returned to the palace where everyone was delighted that the young couple were to be married and become the future king and queen.

The Three Furies

Orpheus and Eurydice

CHRISTOPH WILLIBALD
VON GLUCK

Orpheus

Eurydice

Amor - God of Love

Christoph
Willibald
von Gluck
1714-1787

The story of Orpheus and Eurydice *is set in ancient Greece and based on a Greek myth. Orpheus was a musician, from the city of Thrace. He lived in a time when the gods and goddesses ruled the world and sometimes came down from their home on Mount Olympus to mingle with humankind. Orpheus was one of their favourite mortals. Whether he sang, or played his lyre, he made such sweet music that no one and nothing could resist it.*

Orpheus's music was not just useful for entertainment. When the Greek hero Jason took his ship, the Argo, *on a journey to capture the golden fleece, Orpheus went with him to calm the winds and the waves. And Jason's companions, the Argonauts, would have gone to their deaths, lured by the exquisite voices of the treacherous sea-maidens called the Sirens, had it not been for Orpheus. He sang so melodiously that the Sirens stopped singing to listen to him and the sailors lived to have other adventures.*

Orpheus was married to a beautiful nymph, also from Thrace, called Eurydice and they were very happy. Then one day, Eurydice went for a walk by the river where she was seen by a god called Aristaeus who began to chase her. As she ran away from him, Eurydice stepped on a snake and was bitten. The snake was poisonous and its venom killed Eurydice.

The gods punished Aristaeus but that did not help Orpheus who still had to face life without his beloved wife. He was deeply saddened by her death and did not know how he would go on. It was hard to understand that someone so sweet and kind as Eurydice could die so young.

Orpheus's music, which normally had such power, seemed to be impotent in the presence of death. So, at last, he laid her to rest on a shrine of leaves and flowers so that he and his friends could say a final farewell to the beautiful Eurydice.

Christoph Gluck's father was a forester, and young Gluck left home when he was fourteen to study music in Prague, now the capital of the Czech Republic. He wrote his first opera when he was twenty-seven.

Orpheus and Eurydice

CHRISTOPH WILLIBALD VON GLUCK

Eurydice had died and all her friends were mourning her. Why Eurydice, they lamented. Why did the snake have to bite her? She was too young to die. Besides, who had she ever harmed? Her husband Orpheus could bear it no longer. The same questions ran through his mind too, and he needed to be alone with his grief.

Orpheus's friends understood and faded silently away, leaving him to say goodbye in peace. Orpheus took out his lyre and began to play. His music was so beautiful, it was said to have power over the beings of all three worlds: Mount Olympus, home of the gods; Earth and sea, where humans and animals lived; and the Underworld where the dead went.

Orpheus wept and called to Eurydice to come back but it is a rule of the God of Death that he never returns anyone he has claimed. So, though Orpheus sang songs and played pleading music, Eurydice showed no sign of coming back to life.

At last, Orpheus gave up trying to awaken her. He knelt before her body for the very last time and bent his head in final farewell. As he did so, a song of prayer was torn out of him. He sang:

Gods of the Underworld,
You who guard the Underworld for Pluto,
The great God of Death,
The one who never changes his mind!
Please, please let me come into your world.
Let me convince you
That Eurydice belongs back on Earth,
With me.

Let me see for myself
If my longing is as strong
As your will.

All at once, Orpheus's song was interrupted by a voice he had never heard before.

'I am Amor,' announced the voice. 'I am the God of Love. I bring you a message from the gods. The law forbids any living mortal to cross the boundaries of the Underworld but, in spite of this, they have decided to grant your prayer. You may journey into the Land of the Dead. If you can persuade its guardians to let you find Eurydice and bring her back to Earth with you, then she will return.'

'You mean she can come back from the dead?' gasped Orpheus, amazed. 'Is it really possible?'

'Anything is possible,' laughed Amor. 'It's true, you know, that your music can bend the most determined will. But there is a price.'

'Anything,' promised Orpheus, 'as long as you give me the chance to have Eurydice back.'

'Well then, remember, once you have found Eurydice and begun the journey home, you must not look at her or speak to her. If you do, you'll lose her for ever. Now, good luck. Be brave and, whatever happens, don't lose hope and don't complain.'

Orpheus set off on his quest full of courage and determination. There was lightness in his heart and a spring in his step. Though he knew he had set himself a task that was near impossible, he was grateful to the gods that they had given him this chance.

Very few mortals had ever managed to reach the Underworld. Even fewer had succeeded in returning to Earth. The River Styx divided the world of the living from the world of the dead. Its dark, deep waters were muddy and thick with reeds, which wound around Orpheus's boat and pulled, making his journey slow and treacherous. But Orpheus toiled on until he reached the other side of the river.

There, chained to the gates of the Underworld, stood the ferocious dog,

Cerberus. Anyone who wanted to reach the Underworld had first to win him over. Beside him waited the Furies, three terrifying sisters whose job it was to decide where the souls of the dead should go. As they saw Orpheus, a living man, approach, they howled loudly in protest, 'NO!' and the souls of the dead clustered around them and joined in their shrieks. 'NO! NO! NO!'

'Who is this audacious human who dares to enter the terrible Land of the Dead?' screamed the Furies.

'Why have you come to this miserable place?' cried the ghosts.

'Aren't you afraid of Cerberus?' screamed the Furies. 'Can't you see he guards the Underworld?'

Orpheus looked at Cerberus. He was a horrifying sight, no ordinary dog, but a monstrous creature with three great heads that growled and snapped and snarled, all at the same time. But Orpheus was so determined to get on with his quest that not even Cerberus frightened him. He lifted his lyre and struck a note which turned into more notes until his fingers on the strings made the music flow. It sounded like the sad, lonely streams that rush high in the mountains or deep in the woods without ever joining up with one another. Then he explained to Cerberus and the Furies that he was on a quest.

'Eurydice, my wife, is dead and the gods have given me the chance to get her back. But as the guardians of the Underworld, only you, the Furies, can permit me to enter the Realm of the Dead. I know,' Orpheus added, 'that your rules are very strict and I do not intend to go against your wishes. But I had to come and see you to beg you myself before I gave up hope of taking Eurydice back.'

'Well,' said the Furies, wondering what it was about Orpheus that was making them want to be kind. 'We are feeling quite sorry for you.' It was strange for them to feel this way, all soft and warm inside, and they quite liked it. So they talked amongst themselves and agreed that Orpheus was not just a very talented musician but a very brave and determined man to come and face them.

'We have decided to do something we have never done before and are not very likely to do ever again,' they said, smiling rather rustily. 'We are going to let you into the Realm of the Dead where no living being goes and from which no dead soul departs.'

Then the Furies raised their voices and threw up their arms. 'Open the gates,' they commanded, 'and let the mortal enter! He has won our hearts.'

And as the gates opened and Orpheus walked through, the Furies were quite overcome and did something else they had rarely done before. They danced. Oh, how they whirled, swayed and spun, and as they did so, they sent their good wishes with the lonely young man.

Orpheus wandered through the Underworld, alert for sight or sound of Eurydice. What he saw around him was not always pleasant and he would sometimes have preferred not to look at all. But who knew where he would find Eurydice? There were people here who had done dreadful deeds and their punishments were just as horrifying. They screamed in pain and moaned so loudly that at times Orpheus felt he could not bear their torture any more. Then he took up his lyre and soothed their anguish with his gentle music. But death comes to all of us, not just to the evil, and Orpheus believed that there must be places set aside for those who had lived good lives.

'That must be where Eurydice is,' Orpheus thought to himself. 'If only I could find her.'

Determined as ever, he wandered on until he reached the Elysian fields at the centre of the Underworld, where the purest souls lived. There, in the distance, he could hear the contented spirits. They sang of the meadows of happiness; of their blissful existence; and of how they were never sad, ill or troubled. Orpheus tried to look more closely, but the light was so strong that it dazzled his eyes. All he could see was the dance of the souls as they flitted round in a circle, celebrating their tranquillity.

'What a pure and powerful light,' Orpheus thought, 'and what exquisite music.'

He stood still for a moment, smelling the fragrance of the breeze and listening to the tinkle of a stream. Everything he saw and heard felt calm — except his own mind. 'And that,' he thought sadly, 'will never be peaceful again, unless Eurydice comes home with me.'

65

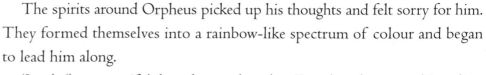

The spirits around Orpheus picked up his thoughts and felt sorry for him. They formed themselves into a rainbow-like spectrum of colour and began to lead him along.

'Look for your wife,' they chorused, and to Eurydice they sang, 'Eurydice, go to your husband. Life on Earth doesn't compare with the peace we find here, but if you love him as much as he loves you, you will be happy with him wherever you are.'

Orpheus could hardly believe what he was hearing. These spirits were actually speaking to Eurydice. Any moment now, he would be able to speak to her too, and see her and … suddenly, Amor's words echoed in his ears. 'Remember, when you find Eurydice and begin the journey home, you must not look at her or speak to her. If you do, you'll lose her for ever.'

'Is it you, Eurydice?' he asked, averting his gaze. 'Is it really you?'

'It is really me, Orpheus,' Eurydice replied, softly.

'I've come to take you home,' Orpheus said. Eurydice reached out and took Orpheus's hand.

'Let's go home,' he urged, turning away quickly. He longed to look at Eurydice but he was terrified of breaking the conditions set by the gods. Without a word, he led her through a thick forest, upwards over the slope of a mountain and into a cave. Outside the cave was another forest. Eurydice fell back a little. She was getting tired. Orpheus longed to stop and let her rest, to comfort her and talk to her. But he knew he must not. Terrified of breaking the conditions, he ploughed on, faster and faster, dragging Eurydice along, so that they could soon be back on Earth where he could look at her and speak to her.

'Why won't you look at me, Orpheus?' Eurydice complained, puzzled by Orpheus's odd behaviour. Orpheus dropped Eurydice's hand.

It was becoming harder and harder for him not to reassure her and he was afraid he would not be strong enough. He could hear the hurt in her voice as she asked, 'Why are you letting go of my hand?'

Orpheus did not answer. 'I know,' thought Eurydice, 'that Orpheus has gone through dangers and ordeals to take me home. But why won't he look at me?'

Of course, she did not know about the condition made by the gods. She did not know that if Orpheus turned around even once, they would be separated from each other for ever. And she did not know that every time she asked him a question or made a complaint, Orpheus came closer to losing her.

'You could at least sit down a moment and speak to me,' coaxed Eurydice. 'You came all the way to the Realm of the Dead to find me. And I'm truly touched – enough to leave my peaceful new home. I'll go with you anywhere, Orpheus, you know I will. But do you still love me?'

'Of course I love you,' Orpheus thought silently, 'but I can't tell you yet. Please, please, be patient and everything will be all right very soon.'

Naturally, Eurydice could not read Orpheus's mind. She grew more and more hurt by his silence.

'I think you are being very rude and cruel,' she grumbled, at last. 'You've come to fetch me but you won't say a word. Perhaps you think your journey was not worth the trouble, after all. Orpheus! Look at me!'

Orpheus longed to turn and speak to her but walked stubbornly on, listening to her footsteps behind him, imagining her walking close to him. He noticed Eurydice's voice was beginning to tremble. He prayed hard for the strength not to turn around to see how she was doing.

'Just a little longer,' he told himself, clenching his fists, 'and I'll have her back for good.' But the sound of Eurydice's footsteps seemed to get further away and fade.

'I don't think you love me anymore,' Orpheus heard Eurydice say, in a faint, distant voice. 'And if that's the case, I think I'd rather be dead and stay here.'

'No!' cried Orpheus, as her footfall faded away altogether. 'No, Eurydice, you mustn't think that! Of course I love you.'

He rushed back and held her in his arms. The next moment, Eurydice crumpled and slid to the ground. Orpheus had broken his word – he had failed his test. Now, he would never see Eurydice again.

'This time she's gone for ever,' cried Orpheus. 'What have I done?' He fell to his knees beside her.

'Eurydice, answer me,' he begged. But Eurydice remained silent.

'She can't hear me,' groaned Orpheus. 'Please, Eurydice, wait for me. If you can't come back to life, I'll die too. Then we can be together.'

Orpheus took out his knife and was about to stab himself, when a voice rang out.

'Stop, Orpheus! Listen to me.'

'Who are you?' shouted Orpheus. 'How dare you interfere?'

'I am Amor, the God who watches over you.'

Orpheus hung his head, ashamed that he had failed to fulfil Amor's hopes.

'Why bother with me?' he asked, miserably. 'I've let you down.'

Amor laughed. 'I've come to say that you can have Eurydice back. We gods have decided you have suffered enough and you've proved your love and courage. We want to reward you.'

From their home on Mount Olympus, the gods and goddesses looked down at Orpheus with pity and affection. But, of course, he could not see them. He watched, feeling wretched, as Amor reached out and touched Eurydice's lifeless body. To Orpheus's amazement, she stirred and sat up. The next moment, they were hugging each other and laughing with joy and excitement.

'How good you are to me, you gods. How can Eurydice and I ever thank you enough?' Orpheus said, happily.

'Just carry on believing in us and do as we say and be good to each other,' chuckled Amor, turning to go. 'Oh, and get out of this deathly place as fast as you can, won't you?'

Solokha~ a Widow, thought to be a Witch

The Devil

Christmas Eve

NIKOLAI RIMSKY-KORSAKOV

Panas

The village Priest

The mayor of Dikanka

Chub~ an old Cossack

Oksana~ Chub's daughter

Vakula ~ a blacksmith son of Solokha

Patsyuk a Wizard

The Tsarina Empress of Imperial Russia

Nikolai
Rimsky-Korsakov
1844~1908

The story of Christmas Eve *is set in eighteenth-century Ukraine. It is based on a short story by the imaginative nineteenth-century Russian writer, Nikolai Gogol, and spiced with local beliefs and customs handed down over the centuries.*

The opera tells the story of Vakula, the blacksmith, and his sweetheart Oksana, daughter of the retired Cossack, Chub. Oksana sends Vakula on a dangerous quest. Determined to return successful, Vakula forces the Devil to help him and by doing so he unwittingly changes the fate of the world. Unknown to him, a much bigger victory is at stake: the battle of night and day, of spring and winter and of good and evil is being fought that very night.

In Slav mythology, the sun sleeps from the solstice (December 25) until the Russian Christmas Day (January 7), and evil spirits use this time of darkness to make mischief. It is Christmas Eve as the opera begins and the people of Dikanka are rejoicing because tomorrow is Christmas Day, a time of peace, when Jesus was born and brought goodwill to the world, and because the sun will rise once more. Only Solokha, the widow, is not celebrating, as she is really a witch.

While the priest finishes the service and prepares a feast for the village elders, Solokha keeps an appointment with the Devil. They have urgent matters to discuss. They cannot stand the merry-making of Christmas. How can they change all this happiness into misery and despair? How can they ensure that spring is banished for ever, that day never dawns again and that the world is ruled for evermore by the Powers of Evil? As this is the last day of darkness, Solokha and the Devil must act swiftly if they are to stop Christmas Day coming. This is their last chance for another year to hatch their wicked plots.

Nikolai Rimsky-Korsakov did not have a musical background — he was an officer in the Russian Navy — but another composer encouraged him to write music. He taught himself and wrote many fairy-tale operas, full of the folk songs he loved to collect.

Christmas Eve

NIKOLAI RIMSKY-KORSAKOV

Across the rooftops of the Ukrainian village of Dikanka, the Devil and Solokha, the widow, were discussing the state of the world. They were not in good spirits. It was getting so that no one feared the Devil anymore. Just the other day, Solokha's son Vakula, the blacksmith, had painted a picture of the Devil being rolled out of the village in a barrel. Tonight was Christmas Eve and everyone would soon be out singing carols.

'I hate Christmas,' griped the Devil. 'It means spring is round the corner and everything's going to be light and bright.'

'All the harder to do our evil deeds,' agreed Solokha.

The Devil looked down and saw Vakula waiting outside the cottage of Chub, the Cossack, and his daughter Oksana. He smiled horribly. 'I'll steal the moon. I'll pitch the world into darkness and your oafish son will be too scared to visit his sweetheart, Oksana.'

'Vakula isn't scared of the dark, you know,' Solokha said, puzzled.

'No, but he is scared of Oksana's father,' the Devil sniggered. 'Chub won't go far in a blizzard.'

'Ooooh! I like it. Then I can have Chub for myself. The richest man in Dikanka. Now, here's the plan: you stick the moon in your pocket and I'll shove the stars in my apron. We'll brew up a blizzard, cover the cottages in snow and keep Oksana and Vakula apart.'

'Let's do it!' yelled the Devil as they soared into the sky.

Down in the village, old Panas staggered out of a tavern. He was on his way to visit the priest and had promised to collect Chub. He fixed his bleary eyes on the moon, then blinked hard. Surely not? But yes! A silhouette was flying towards the moon. Panas wished he hadn't eaten those pickled herrings

71

– true, they were delicious but they did nasty things to his stomach – and now, it seemed, to his eyes too. He looked again. Now the moon was shaking.

The wind howled and he pulled his coat closer just as the moon jerked violently and disappeared. Everything went black. The wind howled on and Panas howled into it.

'You can't do that! The moon belongs to everyone. Give it BACK!'

Buckets of snow flew around and settled in piles. Panas ran to Chub's cottage and knocked frantically.

'Someone's stolen the moon,' he gibbered when Chub answered.

'That's bad,' grumbled Chub. 'Well, it's either the Devil or the council and since we can do nothing about it, let's get on to the priest.'

So they plodded into the blizzard, warming themselves with thoughts of the priest's fine food and vodka. But it was not long before Chub decided that he would rather smoke his pipe in front of his own fire than battle the storm. He pulled his coat over his neck and returned to the cottage, brushing a big man in the dark. 'Either that's Vakula the blacksmith trying to pluck up the courage to see Oksana,' thought Chub, 'or I've come to the wrong house.'

'Why are you prowling around here?' Vakula demanded.

Chub did not want to be on the receiving end of the blacksmith's fiery temper. 'Don't be angry,' he said, pitching his voice high so that Vakula did not recognise him. 'I'm singing carols to the gorgeous Oksana.'

'Go carol to the Devil!' snapped Vakula. 'Or you'll be in trouble.'

'Don't you threaten me, you bully,' retorted Chub, forgetting his high voice, then quickly resuming it. 'It's Christmas.'

Vakula shoved Chub roughly aside and the Cossack considered hitting back but decided against it.

If Vakula was out here, he thought craftily, then Solokha was alone at home. What a chance to woo her without the blacksmith breathing down his neck!

As Chub loped off, Vakula's thoughts returned to Oksana. He thought of her bright eyes and her rich laughter. Vakula had to ask her to marry him, even

72

if she only laughed at him. He had practised what to say and now it was time to say it. Determined, Vakula strode in.

Oksana turned from the mirror where she had been admiring herself.

'Where's my wedding chest?' she demanded.

'It's not quite ready,' gulped the enormous man, scared as a child. 'You see, it took a lot more iron than I expected. And I'm painting it all over so that it's fit for a tsarina. But can I stay for a while . . . ?'

'Do what you like,' yawned Oksana. 'I don't care.' A look of curiosity crept on to her face. 'Is it true that your mother is a witch?'

Vakula shifted uneasily. 'What does it matter? All I know is she's my mother. You're the one that matters. If the tsar offered to grant me a single wish, I'd ask for you.'

Vakula's speech was interrupted as a group of girls burst in.

'Are you coming with us, Oksana?' asked one, daintily pointing her toe.

'What lovely slippers, Odanka!' exclaimed Oksana. 'Your boyfriend is not just handsome, he gives you perfect presents!'

'I can get you a pretty pair of shoes, Oksana,' ventured Vakula. 'Just tell me what you want.'

'Not horse-shoes,' replied Oksana, snootily. 'I want the finest shoes in the world – well, at least as fine as the tsarina's and worked all over in gold and silver.'

The girls were in stitches around Oksana. 'She doesn't want much for Christmas, does she?' they joked.

'Get me slippers like that and I'll marry you,' said Oksana.

'Go on,' teased the others. 'On your horse! Get Oksana her slippers.'

Vakula was in no mood to joke. If this was the way to win Oksana, he'd get the slippers. But it would be hard. He set off home with a heavy heart, to say good-bye to his mother.

At home in her hut, Solokha felt grumpy. Getting all those stars to fit in her small apron had been hard enough, but then she'd lost them all through a hole. And Vakula was probably proposing to Oksana after all.

'We didn't do too well, did we?' she whined to the Devil, who was sitting inside the oven to get warm.

'Well, can I help it?' he snarled. 'My hands are warmed on the fires of hell. The moon was freezing. I lost my grip. My fingers were like ice. We could still do some rotten things, though.'

'Like chasing away the light!'

'And frightening children!'

'And making the food and drink go sour!'

They grabbed each other and danced about the hut. The exercise was just getting their blood circulating nicely, when there was a knock on the door.

'Quick!' hissed Solokha. 'In here!' She held up a sack. The Devil climbed in and Solokha tied up the bag. Then she opened the door and let in the mayor.

'Oh Solokha, my beauty,' burbled the mayor. 'I was on my way to the priest when I thought of you, all alone on Christmas Eve. Forget the priest and his party, I thought. I'd rather be with poor, lonely Solokha.'

Before Solokha could answer, there was another knock on the door. 'Hide me, Solokha!' begged the mayor. 'I should be with the priest!'

Solokha found another sack and the mayor climbed in.

This time the priest was calling. 'Solokha, my dear,' he muttered, 'I'd have come earlier, only I was expecting a few people after the evening service.'

The priest was interrupted by a third knock. Solokha hid him in a sack and opened the door to Chub.

'All alone?' asked Chub, teasing. 'Or have you any guests hidden away?'

'No, of course not,' said Solokha, looking uneasily at the row of sacks by her fire. 'Well, it's very nice to be here,' said Chub, singing a jolly tune. But

Solokha could not enjoy his singing because she could hear Vakula calling.

Chub's voice froze in his throat. 'Hide me, Solokha. I'm still bruised from my last meeting with Vakula.'

Swiftly Solokha put Chub into a sack and began stirring a pot on the stove.

Vakula walked through the door and wiped his feet. As he shook the snow from his great body, he saw the sacks by the fire. 'The house will be neater for Christmas if I put these sacks of food outside,' he thought, 'and it will keep them nice and cold.' He lifted up all four and stepped back out of the house.

The village square was alive with people as Vakula watched from his yard.

Girls and boys sang carols and received gifts of food. Old villagers clowned about with the young. Snowballs swished and whizzed past people's ears.

Vakula looked sadly at Oksana having fun, with not a thought in her head about him. He didn't know if he'd ever find her slippers, but one thing he did know, he would not be back without them. He laid down all but one sack and slipped silently away.

'What's that?' asked the girls catching sight of the sacks. Everyone crowded around, curious. Were the bags filled with pies and sausages? Or a side of mutton, an ox, a herd of pigs, a flock of geese?

'Let's look inside,' suggested someone.

The crowd flowed cautiously towards the sacks and someone untied the largest one. Slowly, Chub came out, stretching, as if he'd woken from a long, deep sleep.

'Sorry I'm not a sausage,' he said, 'but maybe there's one in another bag.'

The two other bags opened and the crowd split their sides laughing as the priest and the mayor crawled out and stood, shamefaced, beside Chub.

'I only went in because I saw a light,' lied the priest. 'Everything else was dead dark.'

'I needed to shelter from the storm,' fibbed the mayor.

'Same here,' said Chub.

Everyone knew these were just excuses but it was Christmas and so they forgave them and, as usual, everyone blamed the witch. It was Solokha who lured men into her hut to get hold of their wealth. And what power had they, mere mortals, against the wily witch, the wild and wicked Solokha?

The cheerful village songs of Dikanka were still ringing in Vakula's ears as far, far away, he entered the cottage of the powerful wizard, Patsyuk.

'Excuse me, sir,' he began, staring, amazed, at Patsyuk who sat cross-legged on the floor with his mouth open. 'I want to find the Devil.'

'Then go to the Devil,' said Patsyuk, opening his mouth wide again to let a stream of enchanted dumplings fly in.

'Greedy monkey,' Vakula thought, 'he's getting fatter by the minute. It's disgusting!' But aloud, he implored, 'I'll give you sausages and, look, here is a sack of flour. I'll shoe your horse. Just help me find the Devil.'

'The Devil's riding on your shoulder,' retorted Patsyuk. 'Open the sack.'

Vakula did as he was told and out popped the Devil. Vakula was terrified. 'Get out, you fiend from hell,' he shouted.

'Stop panicking, will you?' snapped the Devil. 'Why are you shouting? I'll give you what you want. You can be rich and marry Oksana.' He pulled out a piece of paper. 'Just sign here.'

'Whatever you say,' said Vakula, slyly. 'Shall I sign in blood?'

The Devil extended his contract, delighted. But instead of signing it, Vakula reached out and grabbed his neck.

'Let me go,' yelped the Devil, kicking his legs in the air. 'Put me down, you big brute!'

'Change yourself into a horse and fly me to the palace of the great tsarina,' commanded Vakula, showing the cowering Devil the crucifix he kept in his shirt.

The Devil obeyed, flying him through the sky, past the moon, stars and planets. Then suddenly, the clouds banked together in mounds and the stars disappeared behind them. Only the moon held her place, shining through the haze so that swirls of airy spirit creatures showed through like flitting shadows. The battle of winter and spring had begun. Patsyuk entered in a flying cauldron, followed by witches and wizards, clanging and banging and flailing their weapons. Together they cast spells and performed ritual dances to defeat light so that the world would be dark for ever.

Leaving the embattled skies, Vakula arrived at the palace of the tsarina and waited as she entered leading a procession of beautifully dressed ladies, courtiers and brightly uniformed soldiers. When they had finished singing her praises, Vakula saw his chance and stepped forward.

'Your Royal Highness,' he said, kneeling at her feet, 'I know it's rude, I mean, staring at your feet like that ... but your slippers are so lovely. There's not a single shoemaker or jeweller in the Ukraine who could create such beautiful shoes. What am I to do? Oksana won't marry me if I can't find some just like them.'

'Stand up,' commanded the tsarina and Vakula rose.

'I've got stacks and stacks of the finest slippers in all the world.' She turned to one of her courtiers. 'Fetch the best pair in my collection. I like this blacksmith. He's honest and direct and it's not often I meet people like him.'

When the slippers arrived, the tsarina handed them to Vakula. 'Give them to your fiancée, with our blessing.'

Vakula bowed deeply, thanking the tsarina from his heart, then he leapt on the Devil's back and rode off.

The night sky was like a great battlefield, strewn with weapons, and the 'Morning Star' and other constellations gleamed brightly. Dawn had won the battle and shone rosily through the smoke from the chimneys of Dikanka. Vakula heard the sweet singing of the congregation and the chiming of church bells. But he sped past on his way to Chub's cottage to see Oksana.

'Vakula the blacksmith has hanged himself,' a woman said, spotting Oksana.

'Have you heard?' babbled another woman, rushing over. 'The blacksmith drowned himself – in the village pond!'

'I don't believe it!' Oksana shuddered, slipping inside her cottage. But the women continued arguing.

'He's hanged himself!'

'He's drowned himself!'

'You're a liar!'

'You're a fool!'

Oksana did not know what to think. One moment she believed Vakula would come back, the next she felt she had sent him to his death. If only she had not been so snooty. If only she had known before sending him off that she loved him! If only he'd come back. Oksana looked longingly at the gate and screamed with delight. Vakula was standing there with a pair of slippers in his hand.

'The blacksmith!' yelped Chub. 'Are you a ghost, sent by the Devil?'

'No,' replied Vakula, 'though I could tell you a thing or two about him. But for now, I want your permission to marry Oksana. I have gifts for you and here are the slippers she wanted. Let me marry her, please.'

For a fleeting moment Chub was sorry he could not marry Solokha if he let Oksana marry Vakula – but what did it matter? Solokha was a witch, after all, and he was better off without her.

'Of course you can marry Oksana,' he laughed.

So Vakula stepped forward and offered her the tsarina's slippers.

'They're beautiful,' whispered Oksana, 'but I'd have married you even without them.'

Well, there was great rejoicing in Dikanka at their wedding and everyone wanted to hear the story of Vakula's quest for the slippers. But Vakula insisted that he forged metal and would leave the writing of stories to Panko, the village story-teller.

'And if you want to know about my visit to the tsarina,' he smiled, 'you must read the story he tells about this Christmas Eve.'

Notes

BRITTEN, BENJAMIN (1913-1976)
British composer, pianist and conductor

Eric Crozier, the librettist, and Benjamin Britten put together the story for *The Little Sweep* in one afternoon. It was inspired by two of William Blake's poems. The characters were based on children both men knew and Iken Hall really existed in Great Glemham, Suffolk.

First performed: Aldeburgh, June 1949.

The Little Sweep
Alleyn School Choir, English Group Orchestra / Benjamin Britten
(Decca/London CD 436392)

MOZART, WOLFGANG AMADEUS (1756-91)
Austrian composer

Not long before Mozart died, when he was only thirty-five years old, he threw his last energies into completing *The Magic Flute*. Emanuel Schikaneder, the librettist, and Mozart found it a very difficult piece to write since they had to be careful about what they said. They belonged to a secret society, called the Freemasons, which the rulers of Austria feared was against the Church and even the country. Some thought that the Queen of Night in the opera was meant to be the Empress Maria-Theresa or the Church. Mozart and Schikaneder had to keep cutting and rewriting parts of it so as not to break the law. But when it was eventually performed, just a couple of months before Mozart died, it was a triumph.

First performed: Vienna, 30 September 1791.

The Magic Flute (Die Zauberflöte)
Vienna Boys Choir, Vienna State Opera Choir, Vienna Philharmonic Orchestra / Sir George Solti (Decca 433 210-2)
Drottingham Court Theatre Choir / Arnold Ostman (L'Oiseau-Lyre 440-085-2)

HUMPERDINCK, ENGELBERT (1854-1921)
German composer

Humperdinck's first opera *Hänsel and Gretel* was his most popular and successful. The librettist Adelheid Wette based the script on a fairy tale from the Grimm Brothers' collection. As well as writing fresh songs, Humperdinck set some traditional German folksongs to tunes for this piece. Many of them are sung in Germany to this day. But it is not all light-hearted. Humperdinck was a follower of Wagner and some parts of the opera echo Wagner's passionate style.

First performed: Weimar, 23 December 1893.

Hänsel and Gretel
Bavarian Radio Symphony Orchestra, Tolz Boys' Choir / Jeffrey Tate
(EMI CDS7 54022-2)
Cologne Opera Children's Chorus, Cologne Gurzenich Orchestra / John Pritchard
(Sony M2K 79217)

WAGNER, RICHARD (1813-83)
German composer and writer

Wagner usually wrote his own libretti. After losing his job as a conductor in the Russian Orchestra, he was unable to pay his debts. He ran away to Paris and that was where he wrote a shorter version of the opera *The Flying Dutchman*. The director of the Paris Opera paid him 500 francs for the story but wanted someone else to write the music. With the money, Wagner developed it into an excellent full-length opera. The opening scene of a raging sea recalls a violent storm that Wagner himself was caught in when sailing to England.

First performed: Dresden, 2 January 1843.

The Flying Dutchman (Der Fliegende Holländer)
BBC Chorus, New Philharmonia Orchestra / Otto Klemperer
(EMI CMS7 63344-2)
Vienna Philharmonic Orchestra, Vienna State Opera Choir / Christoph von Donyani (Decca 436 418-2)

ROSSINI, GIOACCHINO (1792-1868)
Italian composer

Rossini was one of the greatest composers of comic opera. His very successful *La Cenerentola* was based on the fairy tale *Cinderella*, originally written in French by Charles Perrault. The librettist, Jacopo Ferretti, left out the fairy godmother and all the magical transformations, such as the pumpkin turning into a carriage. Not only would the special effects have been very difficult to produce in 1817, but Rossini did not like supernatural things.

First performed: Rome, 17 January 1817.

La Cenerentola
Chorus and Orchestra of Teatro Communale, Bologna / Riccardo Chailly
(Decca 436 902-2)
Scottish Opera Chorus, London Symphony Orchestra / Claudio Abbado,
(Deutsche Grammophon 423 861-2GHZ)

GLUCK, CHRISTOPH WILLIBALD VON (1714-87)
German composer

Gluck wrote forty-six operas, but *Orpheus and Eurydice* is his most famous work. The librettist Ranieri de' Calzabigi based the story on the Greek myth, but he gave it a happy, rather than tragic, ending. At first the part of Orpheus in Gluck's opera was written for a castrato. Such voices are impossible to find today and so Orpheus is sometimes a contralto (a woman with a very deep voice). Today a tenor usually sings the part in the traditional voice of a hero. In fact Gluck himself adapted it for a tenor when the piece was performed in Paris in 1774.

First performed: Vienna, 5 October 1762.

Orpheus and Eurydice (Orfeo ed Euridice)
Stuttgart Chamber Choir, Tafelmusik / Frieder Bernius (Sony Classical Vivarte SK 48040)
(*Orphee et Eurydice*) Lyon Opéra, Monteverdi Choir / John Eliot Gardiner
(EMI CDS7 49834-2)

RIMSKY-KORSAKOV, NIKOLAI (1844-1908)
Russian composer

Rimsky-Korsakov composed 15 operas. *Christmas Eve* (1895) almost never reached the stage because a Grand Duke, who watched a dress-rehearsal, was offended that anyone could perform the part of the tsarina. He was sure the tsarina was based on the Empress Catherine II. When the Emperor heard the story, he also banned a set showing the tsar's palace. Before the opera could be performed, Rimsky-Korsakov had to agree to change the tsarina's part for that of a male courtier.

First perfomed: St Petersburg, 10 December 1895.

Christmas Eve (with May Night)
Yurlov Academia Choir, Moscow Forum Theatre Orchestra / M. Yurovsky
(Harmonia Mundi CMX 388054)

BAREFOOT BOOKS publishes high-quality picture books for children of all ages and specialises in the work of artists and writers from many cultures. If you have enjoyed this book and would like to receive a copy of our current catalogue, please contact our London office —

tel: 0171 704 6492   fax: 0171 359 5798

e-mail: sales@barefoot-books.com

website: www.barefoot-books.com